MAKE YOUR B

Business Agility is an approach that gives the right business flexibility and fast decision-making in a volatile environment, providing a great capacity for innovation, adaptation and change. Businesses everywhere are trying to 'get business agile' – but it's not easy to adjust to becoming this adaptive.

How can conventional organisations succeed in this transformation?

In this book, project and change management expert Peter Taylor walks you through the change process step by step, providing a tried and tested transformation roadmap: benefits are outlined, solutions to common challenges offered, and tried and tested methods and tools provided. He guides you towards a decentralised management style that offers more successful decision making through collaboration.

By reducing processes, adjusting the governance and believing in 'the power of the people' to deliver simple success in a time of complex demand, the guidance in this book will help any manager get Business Agile.

Peter Taylor is a Project Management Expert, Speaker, Author and Consultant. He is also a change expert who has built and led five global PMOs across several industries and has advised many other organisations in transformation strategy. He is the author of the Amazon number 1 bestselling project management book *The Lazy Project Manager*, along with many other books on project leadership, project marketing, project challenges and executive sponsorship. In the last few years, he has delivered over 450 lectures around the world, in over 25 countries.

MAKE YOUR BUSINESS AGILE

A ROADMAP FOR TRANSFORMING YOUR MANAGEMENT AND ADAPTING TO THE 'NEW NORMAL'

Peter Taylor

Routledge
Taylor & Francis Group

LONDON AND NEW YORK

First published 2021
by Routledge
2 Park Square, Milton Park, Abingdon, Oxon OX14 4RN

and by Routledge
52 Vanderbilt Avenue, New York, NY 10017

Routledge is an imprint of the Taylor & Francis Group, an informa business

British Library Cataloguing-in-Publication Data
A catalogue record for this book is available from the British Library

Library of Congress Cataloging-in-Publication Data
Names: Taylor, Peter, 1957- author.
Title: Make your business agile : a roadmap for transforming your management and adapting to the 'new normal' / Peter Taylor.
Description: Abingdon, Oxon ; New York, NY : Routledge, 2021. | Includes bibliographical references and index.
Identifiers: LCCN 2020046169 (print) | LCCN 2020046170 (ebook)
Subjects: LCSH: Organizational change. | Management–Employee participation. | Organizational effectiveness.
Classification: LCC HD58.8 .T393 2021 (print) | LCC HD58.8 (ebook) | DDC 658.4/06–dc23
LC record available at https://lccn.loc.gov/2020046169
LC ebook record available at https://lccn.loc.gov/2020046170

ISBN: 978-0-367-46894-1 (hbk)
ISBN: 978-0-367-74708-4 (pbk)
ISBN: 978-1-003-03182-6 (ebk)

Typeset in Times New Roman
by Taylor & Francis Books

To the 'gang of nine': Ash, Jen, Tor, Georgia, Adam, Sam, Ellie, Scott, and Jaz – be a flamingo in a flock of pigeons.*

* Quote by Savannah Larsen: 'Be a Flamingo in a Flock of Pigeons'

CONTENTS

ACKNOWLEDGEMENTS

This is a book that I could not have written by myself.

I was increasingly interested, intrigued and challenged by this world of 'Business Agility' that I saw some companies achieving, and many others who were seemingly failing at, and believed that there was value in a book about this, to my mind, critical subject. But whilst I had thoughts and insights into many aspects of this world, I have relied heavily on people who just know more than me to provide the real detail and inspiration. And for that, I am profoundly grateful to all of them.

You can read all of their amazing profiles in the 'Valued contributors' chapter at the end of the book but, for now, thank you Emma, Evan, Stephen, Parag and Bentzy.

I could not have done it without you, so thank you.

ABOUT THE AUTHOR

Peter Taylor

Keynote speaker, Consultant, Trainer and Coach, Peter is the author of the number 1 bestselling project management book *The Lazy Project Manager*, along with many other books on Project Management, PMO Development, Executive Sponsorship, Transformation Leadership, and Speaking Skills.

He has delivered over 450 lectures around the world in over 25 countries and has been described as 'perhaps the most entertaining and inspiring speaker in the project management world today'.

Peter Taylor is a prolific author with 20 books published in the last 11 years, his most recent Routledge book *Project Management: It's All Bollocks!* being a huge success!

Peter's key strengths include: Embedding robust governance to ensure successful delivery of £multi-million change programs and working with stakeholders throughout the project lifecycle to ensure delivery of tangible business benefits; as well as introducing best practice processes aligned with an organisation's culture and maturity. Working across multiple industries including Manufacturing, Health, Pharmaceuticals, FMCG, Aerospace, HR, Public Sector, Education and Finance. Deep understanding of the project economy world and internal/external stakeholder interaction. PMO design, build and re-engineering expert. Strong communication skills and the ability to engage effectively at all levels within an organisation, shop-floor to board level.

Business Agility driven business transformation guidance is available if your organisation requires inspiration, insight, and guidance.

Contact Peter: www.thelazyprojectmanager.com

INTRODUCTION

by Evan Leybourn

Sometimes you just have to jump out of the windows and grow wings on the way down

Ray Bradbury, 1995[1]

When Peter asked me to write this introduction, my first draft was a call-to-action; a series of statistics and stories about the increasing rate of company failures and bankruptcies around the world. A thousand words setting the context for the VUCA world[2] we live in today. And yet as I wrote it, it became clear that this book isn't about survival. Survival is just the starting point. No one ever won by racing to the starting point.

Instead, I want you to truly understand that Business Agility isn't about survival; rather Business Agility is what is needed to *thrive*. These are VUCA times – that much is clear. So, what does it take to be a market leader in this environment?

I want you to start by imagining what is possible.

Imagine a company where customer delight is tangible. Where customers advocate and recommend your products and services. Where customer feedback ensures strong product-market fit. This is a company that adapts and, more importantly, shapes changing customer trends.

We are in an age where your customer moves faster than you. And they know more than you.

There is a concept in economics called Information Asymmetry and it is critical in price negotiations. Very simply, the person with the most information controls the price. Once, that was the company. Now, it is the customer.

This fundamentally changes how companies engage with their customers. If you listen to your customers and build products and services that meet their underlying needs – they will stay. And they will bring others to you.

However, if a competitor listens closer or builds it faster, they will find out and they will go.

Next, imagine a company where employees can operate with independence and in the company's best interest. Where they look forward to coming into work. Where they say TGIM, not TGIF.[3]

It is a fact that most of us spend more time working than we do with our family. Whether it's at the office or at home on our laptops and mobiles, work pervades every waking moment. This is not a value judgement – it's neither good nor bad – it just is. However, as work takes up most of our waking life, shouldn't is also be the best part of our life? Empowerment, autonomy, purpose – these aren't just buzzwords sold by management consultants. These are vital to a happy, and thus productive, workforce.

Treat your workforce with respect. Teach your managers how to delegate properly. Truly listen to people during exit interviews as they leave your organisation. Trust them to act in your best interest. Yet accept that mistakes will be made and help them learn how not to make them again. Don't fall into the trap of constraining people with bureaucracy and process and still expecting them to be productive and innovative.

Finally, imagine a company that is both productive and efficient. One that reliably delivers value to the shareholders despite (and sometimes because of) the volatility of the market.

Let us start with a simple fact that many of us have forgotten – you are not in business to make money. You are in business to serve your customer. The better you serve your customer, the more they will buy your products and services, and the more money you will make. Money is an indicator of success, not success itself.

Help shareholders and the board understand the changing expectations of your customers. Enhance your metrics and annual reports to go beyond just the financial health of the company. Foster an open, two-way, relationship between your company's leaders and the board, so you can go after long-term opportunities, as opposed to short-term wins.

This is an organisation where customer obsession creates employee engagement which, in turn, generates shareholder value. In other words, Business Agility – and the only way to survive, and thrive, in an unpredictable marketplace.

Is this the future you want for you and your company? It is not an easy journey and will take much longer than you think. Yet, precisely because it is hard, it is worthwhile. So, get started and, in the immortal words of Ray Bradbury, maybe you'll grow wings along the way.

Evan Leybourn,
Founder of the Business Agility Institute

NOTES

1 Ray Douglas Bradbury was an American author and screenwriter. One of the most celebrated 20th- and 21st-century American writers, he worked in a variety of genres including fantasy, science fiction, horror, and mystery fiction.
2 VUCA – a world of volatility, uncertainty, complexity and ambiguity
3 Thank God it's Monday – Thank God it's Friday

INTRODUCTION

by Peter Taylor

Professor Julian Birkinshaw,[1] Professor of Strategy and Entrepreneurship at the London Business School has suggested that the world is entering something he calls 'The Age of Agile'.

Organisations throughout history, Birkinshaw said in a speech at the Global Peter Drucker Forum in Vienna Austria, were of three types: bureaucracies, meritocracies, and adhocracies.

The age of bureaucracy was where power was through hierarchy and managed by rules, the age of meritocracy was where power was through knowledge and guided by logical argument, but now we are in the age of adhocracy where it is about action, about getting things done, and done fast. Experimentation and outcome achievement are key.

We are, I believe, in the age of the 'Business Agile'. We are also, without doubt, in the VUCA world of volatility, uncertainty, complexity and ambiguity.

> Note: When I first submitted the proposal for this book there was a clear need to win the argument that we lived in a VUCA world with many people, but based on the world's very immediate experiences of global disruption perhaps this argument is one that no longer is required. We have all lived through one of the most impactful worldwide events in our lifetime and what we have collectively experienced ticks all of the boxes of volatility, uncertainty, complexity, and ambiguity.

Covid-19 is truly a Black Swan event experience.[2]

A Black Swan is an unpredictable event that is beyond what is normally expected of a situation and has potentially severe consequences.

Black Swan events are characterised by their extreme rarity, severe impact, and the widespread insistence they were obvious in hindsight (this is already happening).

> Note: That said, within the business world it is perhaps still relevant to put forward this explanation/argument in order to gain the right attention for a change in attitude, behaviour, and focus and a move towards a 'Business Agile' world.

'Business Agile' is the approach of providing greater flexibility and faster decision-making in the modern business world, a world where organisations that aren't Business Agile will take longer to succeed and be less flexible in this modern, demanding business world, and fail at a faster rate potentially.

But that brings about a challenge with regards to supporting this rapidly moving world of change driven through projects.

A world of complexity and criticality with projects ranging across the globe, resources remotely and virtually engaged, and the leaders of change tasked with delivering the best for their organisations whilst those very organisations spin ever faster on their strategic arc.

The answer, it seems, is not to meet complexity with complexity but to meet it with simplicity.

To achieve this 'easy to say yet hard to do' statement I believe that organisations need to look closely at and invest well in the following five key areas.

COLLABORATION

One way to do this is to harvest the power of the 'Hive Mind'.[3]

By harnessing the collective power, thoughts, experience, knowledge and wisdom of the many, rather than the few, better decisions can be made. And by utilising the many business social technological platforms, these more-inclusive decision-making processes can be faster than the more traditional 'meet/discuss/agree/act' physical meetings of the past.

Change leaders today need to embrace this more social, decentralised and collaborative world in order to succeed in the adhocracy age we are well and truly in, right now.

TEAMING

Associated with collaboration is the urgent need for companies to really invest in understanding and developing the teams that work within them. Especially as we progress towards an increasingly project-based economy.[4]

With change being ever constant and with the traditional structures of organisations being to break down through this overlay of project activity then it is clear that teams will be less fixed, less static, and more dynamic. As such, such teams need to reach the performing state (as defined by Bruce Tuckman[5]) faster and faster.

AGILE

Underlying this Business Agility is the requirement for the project-based economy that they exist in and support to be 'agile' in a project sense.

Agile Project Management[6] is an approach via a series of steps that involves delivering value iteratively and incrementally throughout the project life cycle.

And, at the heart of this is a need for absolute collaboration within project teams. I feel we are beginning to see a pattern here.

UNLEARNING

'Unlearning is the process of letting go, reframing and moving away from once useful mindsets and acquired behaviors that were effective in the past, but now limit our success. It is not forgetting, removing, or discarding knowledge or experience; it is the conscious act of letting go of outdated information, and actively engaging in taking in new information to inform effective decision making and action.'[7]

So, if our reality changes (and it clearly has in recent times) then we have got to be open and willing to unlearn our old, outdated mindsets and behaviours if we want to ensure we will continue to stay relevant.

SIMPLICITY

And last, but not least, is the overarching and underlying requirement that whatever a business does it aims to apply KISS[8] at every level.[9]

Reduce the processes, adjust the governance, and believe, really believe, in the power of the people to deliver simple success in a time of complex demand.

If we agree with Professor Julian Birkinshaw that we are in the age of adhocracy where it is about action, about getting things done, and done fast through experimentation and outcome achievement, then we need to harness the collective power of the many through collaboration and high performing teams, driven with an agile mindset, free from traditional constraints and operating in a process world of simplicity.

And your organisation needs to make this cultural mindset change today!

NOTES

1 Julian Birkinshaw FBA, FAcSS is a British academic. He is Professor of Strategy and Entrepreneurship at the London Business School, where he is the Academic Director of the Deloitte Institute of Innovation and Entrepreneurship. He is the author of four books on management.
2 We might even argue the world hit an entire flock of black swans such is the global impact.
3 Hive Mind: a notional entity consisting of a large number of people who share their knowledge or opinions with one another, regarded as producing either uncritical conformity or collective intelligence.
4 A project-based economy is where organisations deliver value to stakeholders through successful completion of projects, delivery of products, and alignment to value streams. And all of these initiatives deliver financial and societal value.
5 Bruce Wayne Tuckman was an American Psychological Researcher who carried out his research into the theory of group dynamics. In 1965, he published a theory known as 'Tuckman's stages of group development'. According to this theory, there are four phases of group development: Forming, Storming, Norming, Performing.

6 Agile project management is an iterative approach to project management which allows you to break large projects down into more manageable tasks tackled in short iterations or sprints. This enables your team to adapt to change quickly and deliver work fast.

7 As defined in his recent bestselling book: *Unlearn Let Go of Past Success to Achieve Extraordinary Results* (2018) by Barry O'Reilly.

8 KISS, an acronym for 'keep it simple, stupid' or 'keep it stupid simple', is a design principle that was noted by the US Navy in 1960.

9 I certainly aim to do this in all my presentations and teaching, and in my books. Simplicity conveys understanding and aids learning.

IT'S A VUCA WORLD OUT THERE

1.1 DOES THIS SOUND LIKE YOU?

Is your business life 'Volatile – Uncertain – Complex – Ambiguous'?

Well don't panic, you are certainly not alone, but you should accept that you are part of the 'VUCA' world today!

VUCA is an acronym originally used by the American Military.[1] It was the response of the US Army War College to the collapse of the USSR in the early 1990s when, suddenly, there was no longer the only enemy, resulting in a need for new ways of seeing and reacting.

VUCA is now extensively used in business circles to recognize the increasingly dynamic and fast-paced business world we live in today. The challenges that VUCA represents are obvious in a world where businesses must react quickly and have the ability to change direction based on fact not fiction.

- Volatility refers to the speed of change in your business, sector, industry, location, etc.
  It is associated with demand variables and market fluctuations and drives businesses to faster changes.
- Uncertainty is about knowing what the future might look like.
  It is associated with the inability to understand what is going on despite any amount of data that has been collected in the past, and this becomes a self-accelerating reality with uncertainty building on uncertainty.
- Complexity refers to the number of factors that need to be taken into consideration when making decisions or plans.

The more complex the world is, the harder it is to try and understand all aspects and their interrelationship with each other.

- Ambiguity refers to a lack of clarity about how to interpret something.

  When there is a lack of clarity in knowledge points and often conflicting possible meanings then translating this into meaningful information can be impossible.

1.2 VOLATILITY

V = Volatility: The nature and dynamics of change, and the nature and speed of change forces and change catalysts.

Meaning: Liable to change rapidly and unpredictably, especially for the worse.

In a Forbes article 'What Does VUCA Really Mean?' Jeroen Kraaijenbrink[2] writes: 'Volatility refers to the speed of change in an industry, market or the world in general. It is associated with fluctuations in demand, turbulence, and short time to markets, and it is well-documented in the literature on industry dynamism. The more volatile the world is, the more and faster things change'.

The key here is speed of change and the variability of that change.

The days of nice 3, 4, 5-year plans are long, long gone; yes, there might be some long-term strategy associated to a vision but not at a detailed planning level. The days of starting a project or program and having a clear view of the business landscape that you have to lead that change across is also long gone. Who knows what might suddenly be needed by the organisation? Change in speed and direction driven by competitors, by the market, by the government, even by the people?

Despite the dictionary meaning of 'Liable to change rapidly and unpredictably, especially for the worse', then such volatility should not be seen as a bad thing and that it automatically leads to a 'worse' situation. Instead that volatility, and associated change, is caused by a real need. It should also be considered that only not keeping pace with the volatile demand is what causes any business situation to worsen.

And so, the question has to be 'How can we prepare ourselves to move at the speed required and to be flexible in our approach in order to meet volatility with stability?'

Understanding the dynamics of change is a great start. What is it that makes change happen, what or who initiates this, and who or how can you overlay that change of the current business activities – in a rapid and realistic manner?

Having a change orientated culture and people ready to behave in a collaborative and Business Agile way is another.

Achieving true stability is probably beyond the possible in the modern business day but accepting a degree of volatility as the 'norm' is an exceptionally good way to view the world as relatively 'stable'.

1.3 UNCERTAINTY

U = Uncertainty: The lack of predictability, the prospects for surprise, and the sense of awareness and understanding of issues and events.

Meaning: Not able to be relied on; not known or definite.

'Uncertainty refers to the extent to which we can confidently predict the future. Part of uncertainty is perceived and associated with people's inability to understand what is going on. Uncertainty, though, is also a more objective characteristic of an environment. Truly uncertain environments are those that don't allow any prediction, also not on a statistical basis. The more uncertain the world is, the harder it is to predict'.[3]

The key here is predictability, or the lack of it, more to the point. We are creatures of habit and whilst we might demand change and expect change, we sure don't want to have to change ourselves and that is all part of the uncertainty model in the VUCA world. The (almost) complete disappearance of any normality or certainty in what we do on a week by week, month by month, basis.

The optimistic would argue that when nothing is sure, everything is possible, which is true; but even the most extremely positive people can tire of constant uncertainty and continuous change that is not under their control.

The right, and only sane, approach to this, instead of trying to fight against it, is to assess how we can embrace it. Because in uncertainty there is opportunity and not accepting such uncertainty will limit such opportunity.

The difficulty we, as humans, have is that our brains are wired to react with fear when we're faced with uncertainty. It is just in our DNA; it is the fight or flight overrides that have always been with us. As uncertainty in a situation increases, then the brain shifts control over to the limbic system where our inbuilt emotions, such as fear, are generated. Basically, change worries us, and uncertain or unplanned change worries us even more.

And so, the question has to be 'How can we prepare ourselves to accept uncertainty and to move this towards certainty?'

Addressing our core and natural reaction against uncertainty is a good place to begin, and then to identifying the positives, the opportunities through the cloud of uncertainty can bring us to a more stable and certain place.

It is about feeling that you are, in actual fact, in some sort of 'control'.

1.4 COMPLEXITY

C = Complexity: The multiplex of forces, the confounding of issues, no cause-and-effect chain and confusion that surrounds organisation.

Meaning: Consisting of many different and connected parts – not easy to analyse or understand; complicated or intricate.

'Complexity refers to the number of factors that we need to take into account, their variety and the relationships between them. The more factors, the greater their variety and the more they are interconnected, the more complex an environment is. Under high complexity, it is impossible to fully analyze the environment and come to rational conclusions. The more complex the world is, the harder it is to analyze'.

With everything seemingly connected to everything else, resulting in a whole messy pile of interconnectedness, what we end up with is a very scary looking piece of perceived 'complexity'. *Harvard Business Review* noted, in an article called 'Learning to Live with Complexity' by Gökçe Surgut and Rita Gunther McGrath,[4] that there are two major problems of complexity (and you do need to know the difference between complicated and complex by the way). They said, 'We've observed two problems commonly faced by managers of complex systems: unintended consequences and difficulty making sense of a situation'.

Unintended consequences: In a complex environment, even small decisions can have surprising effects.

Making sense of a situation: It is exceedingly difficult, if not impossible, for an individual decision maker to see an entire complex system. This is essentially a vantage point problem: It's hard to observe and comprehend a highly diverse array of relationships from any one location.

So, the first concern is along the lines of 'impact any one point and who knows what this might lead to', which is a very worrying situation, many would agree.

The second is that 'nobody can actually see the big picture,' even though we have all been trained for years to 'look at the big picture', which was fine until now, because the picture itself cannot be seen in its entirety or 'complexity', it is perhaps now too big.

And so, the question has to be 'How can we understand what can't, apparently, be viewed?'

Which leads us naturally to the appreciation that alone, we can't. But in the company of the many, in the land of true collaboration, the impossible becomes more than possible, thanks to our colleagues and compatriots at work.

1.4 AMBIGUITY

A = Ambiguity: The haziness of reality, the potential for misreads, and the mixed meanings of conditions; cause-and-effect confusion.

Meaning: Open to more than one interpretation; not having one obvious meaning, not clear or decided.

'Ambiguity refers to a lack of clarity about how to interpret something. A situation is ambiguous, for example, when information is incomplete, contradicting or too inaccurate to draw clear conclusions. More generally it refers to fuzziness and vagueness in ideas and terminology. The more ambiguous the world is, the harder it is to interpret'.

The key here is lack of understanding as a result of lack of information, too much information, or conflicting information.

Paul Gibbons, in *The Science of Successful Organisational Change*[5]*: How Leaders Set Strategy, Change Behavior, and Create an Agile Culture* actually stated that 'Ambiguity is not, today, a lack of data, but a deluge of data'.

Too much information flying at us all from every angle and every source. But even then, often with big chunks missing for any complete appreciation. In my own book *How to Get Fired at the C-Level* I spoke about the fact that many, most, organisations do not truly understand the value of their portfolio of change investment due to misunderstandings, missing data, assumptions and general system inadequacies.

And so, the question has to be 'How can we have all the information that we need to make insightful (and rapid) decisions and how can we gain advantage from wisdom across the organisation to use this well?'

I believe that this too, like the complexity issue, leads us to the realisation that we cannot alone, but we can with many contributions. Gaps in knowledge can be filled by others and clear understanding of what that knowledge means can be gained from a collective that self-corrects, self-regulates and self-balances.

1.4.1 VUCA ON VUCA

In practice, the four terms are both related and feed each other to make for an ever increasing VUCA existence for your business.

It is like the Tower Game where touching one block impacts and is impacted by potentially every other block – get it wrong and the whole tower comes down.

Funny in a game situation, but anything but funny in a work environment!

If it is complex and volatile, then the harder it is to predict and the more uncertain it will be.

Organisations are waking up to the fact that they need to adapt today so they can compete in a fast, ever changing environment. But, as Darwin said, success comes to those who are not the strongest, but the most responsive to change.

Hiding your head in the sand whilst the VUCA world surrounds you will not help, but taking action to become Business Agile will.

The key is to not live with the 'fear' of VUCA but address the challenges it offers and consider 'solutions' that can progress your business to a different landscape.

VUCA can be a good thing, a positive thing if you approach it the right way. It can be used as a catalyst to bringing change in your day-to-day world and to progress your business to a new status.

From:	*To:*
Volatility	Stability
Uncertainty	Certainty
Complexity	Simplicity
Ambiguity	Clarity

A 'Business Agile' mind-set will help bring stability, certainty, simplicity, and clarity to your role and to your business, and help you overcome the challenges in a VUCA world.

NOTES

1 VUCA is an acronym – first used in 1987, drawing on the leadership theories of Warren Bennis and Burt Nanus – to describe or to reflect on the volatility, uncertainty, complexity and ambiguity of general conditions and situations. The US Army War College introduced the concept of VUCA to describe the more volatile, uncertain, complex, and ambiguous multilateral world perceived as resulting from the end of the Cold War. More frequent use and discussion of the term 'VUCA' began from 2002 and has subsequently taken root in emerging ideas in strategic leadership that apply in a wide range of organisations.
2 What Does VUCA Really Mean? Jeroen Kraaijenbrink https://www.forbes.com/sites/jeroenkraaijenbrink/2018/12/19/what-does-vuca-really-mean/
3 What Does VUCA Really Mean? Jeroen Kraaijenbrink https://www.forbes.com/sites/jeroenkraaijenbrink/2018/12/19/what-does-vuca-really-mean
4 Learning to Live with Complexity, by Gökçe Surgut and Rita Gunther McGrath https://hbr.org/2011/09/learning-to-live-with-complexity
5 *The Science of Successful Organisational Change: How Leaders Set Strategy, Change Behavior, and Create an Agile Culture* (Pearson, 2015).

THE RISE OF BUSINESS AGILITY

Peter: As well as appreciating that we are all in a world of VUCA then it is equally important to have some clear(er) definition of what we might mean by 'Business Agile'.

There are so, so many conflicting and confusing terms out there:

- Business Agility
- Organisational Agility
- Enterprise Agility
- Enterprise Business Agility
- Structural Agility
- Process Agility
- Strategy Agility
- Agile Up!

These are just a few of them, I am sure you could come up with some more of your own.

Through my lectures and keynote presentations, writing and discussions I have settled on a term that I feel best serves the cause that I am championing, and that is 'Business Agile' but that is always up for debate with others of course.

That said, I invited Parag Gogate (who is, amongst many other things, co-founder of the London Business Agility Meet-up) to put together what you might call a short history of the rise of 'Business Agility' for me.

2.1 A SIMPLE, VERY SHORT HISTORY

Year 2008: The world of business changed due to global financial crisis.

> The term VUCA (Volatility, Uncertainty, Complexity, Ambiguity) started to be used across the business world especially after the 2008 global financial crisis. This situation brought about increased awareness of the globally interconnected, interdependent, and complex world of business and its fragility).[1]

Year 2020: The world has really changed due to the impact of COVID-19. The world of Business has changed. Business Agile is the only option.

> Read the first paragraph again in the context of the COVID-19 impact. Suddenly, VUCA needs no further explanation but is a reality.

2.2 VUCA AND THE AGILE ORGANISATION

As we have seen, the term VUCA is an acronym that stands for Volatility, Uncertainty, Complexity and Ambiguity. With its origins in the US Army, VUCA is being increasingly used to describe today's rapidly changing complex world, especially in the context of economy and organisations.

Mack et al.[2] (2016) present complexity as a key concept and another three elements as the consequences of complexity. This has been based on theoretical perspectives of systems and complexity theory.

Agility or an agile organisation is often perceived as an answer to address the complexity arising out of operating in a VUCA world. According to a survey conducted by The Economist Intelligence Unit (2009),[3] nearly 90% of the executives believe that organisational agility is critical for business success and is a core differentiator in today's rapidly changing business environment. Rapid decision-making and execution came out to be the top concern (61%) followed by a high-performance culture (44%).

Some 44% of respondents said that midsize organisations have the agility edge over the size and reach of large organisations and the entrepreneurial skill of small firms.

This survey was conducted in 2009 after the financial crisis and it is anybody's guess what the results may look like in 2020!

2.3 THE 'AGILE' CONFUSION AND EVOLUTION

2.3.1 AGILE, AGILE AND AGILITY

There is lot of prevailing confusion between Agile, agile and agility.

These terms are now being used interchangeably often leading to misunderstanding and endless debates.

This also has implications for the way we begin to define a 'Business Agile'.[4]

> Agile (noun) has evolved from software development practices such as DSDM, XP, Scrum etc.
>
> agile (adjective) means able to move quickly and easily, able to think quickly and clearly
>
> Agility (noun) means ability to move quickly and easily, ability to think quickly and clearly

2.3.2 EVOLUTION OF 'AGILE'

Agile movement traces its origins to the Agile Manifesto[5] developed in 2001 where representatives from methodologies such as Extreme Programming, SCRUM[6], DSDM[7], Software Development, Crystal[8], Feature-Driven Development[9], Pragmatic Programming[10] and other software development methodologies met to agree a new way of working.

Together they came up with an Agile Software Development Manifesto with the following values:

- Individuals and interactions over processes and tools
- Working software over comprehensive documentation
- Customer collaboration over contract negotiation
- Responding to change over following a plan

From 2001, all software development frameworks that aligned with these values and principles came to be known as Agile techniques. Over the last two decades, Agile practices and methods were able to help organisations and IT teams deliver successful projects as well as software product development initiatives.

According to Rigby, Sutherland, and Takeuchi (2016),[11] Agile traces its true roots back to fields outside IT. Key influencers have been Francis Bacon's articulation of scientific method in 1620, Walter Shewart's PDSA cycle (Plan-Do-Study-Act) of product and process improvement in 1930, Edward Deming's and Taiichi Ohno's work on developing the Toyota Production System in Japan which laid the foundation for Lean in the 1950s and 1960s and even Fredrick Taylor's scientific management of experimentation in 1911!

There have been other influences from the world of Systems Thinking, Complexity and Design theories.

The word 'Agile' itself was inspired by the book by Goldman, Nagel and Preiss in 1994 called *Agile Competitors and Virtual Organizations: Strategies for Enriching the Customer.*[12]

Agile practices are characterised by iterative, incremental product development delivered by self-organising, collaborative teams, requiring a completely different mindset. The focus is firmly on the customer and delivering value as early as possible. Agile practices are particularly suited to the complex environment that the organisations increasingly find themselves in with adaptability, flexibility and minimising risk being the key advantage to counter that.

Agile's development journey evokes passionate debates among agile and other practitioners (is it an evolution or revolution?). Two things however are clear:

1 Agile's roots extend far beyond information technology
2 Agile's branches will continue to spread to improve innovation processes in nearly every function of every industry.

2.3.3 DEFINING A 'BUSINESS AGILE' – BACK TO THE FUTURE

This is a simple yet difficult task since many different variations of this are prevalent causing confusion but not really offering great clarity for general practitioners.

Organisations can be treated as complex adaptive systems (CAS) exhibiting principles such as self-organisation, complexity, emergence, interdependence, space of possibilities, co-evolution, chaos, and self-similarity.[13]

CAS are contrasted with ordered and chaotic systems by the relationship that exists between the system and the agents which act within it. In an ordered system, the level of constraint means that all agent behaviour is limited to the rules of the system.

In a chaotic system, the agents are unconstrained and susceptible to statistical and other analysis. In a CAS, the system and the agents co-evolve; the system lightly constrains agent behaviour, but the agents modify the system by their interaction with it. This self-organising nature is an important characteristic of CAS; and its ability to learn to adapt, differentiates it from other self-organising systems.

Complexity Theory advocates flatter, more flexible organisations, rather than top-down, command-and-control styles of management. Complexity theory also reveals that individual behaviours and choices are more important than executive plans in an organisation. Instead, individuals are highly impacted by their interrelations with other individuals within the organisation.

The goal is to adapt and endure; the focus is on fixing the whole system rather than its parts; teams are capable of self-organisation and self-regulation; and change as a natural, adaptive process. Systems theory tells us that the traditional, mechanical, model cannot be effective, except in a very stable environment.

Ross Ashby's Law of Requisite Variety, formulated in the 1950s, sets out the necessary relationship between the complexity of the environment, the flexibility of a control system and the specificity of the goals imposed on the system.

The more complex the environment, and the 'tighter' the targets, the more flexibility the control system must have: 'only variety can absorb variety'. Failure to provide 'requisite variety' will result in instability (boom and bust) and ultimately system failure. The only way out is to 'game the system'; artificially injecting flexibility into the system by other means.

Given a complex environment the only way that complex organisations can be successfully controlled is through exploiting the capacity of a system for self-organisation and self-regulation by adopting an organic model.

According to Hoverstadt (2008),[14] the most common organisational model in use is the hierarchical model. It represents the formal power structure of the organisation and fails to model any of the more fundamental things about the organisation – what it is, what it does, how it does it, its processes, formal and informal structures, communications and information transfers, or decision making.

The Viable System Model (VSM) developed by Stafford Beer[15] offers a more sophisticated alternative, one that can be used both for diagnosing existing organisations, and for designing new ones. Beer sought to develop a 'science of organisation', by setting down the principles that underpin all organisations, and create viability, which is the capacity to exist and thrive in sometimes unpredictable and turbulent environments. Hoverstadt further explains that the criteria of viability require that organisations become capable of adapting appropriately to their chosen environment or adapting their environment to suit themselves.

A key concept here is that of complexity and VSM deals with this in two ways:

- By looking at the balance of complexity between different parts of the system, and
- By unfolding in a fractal structure, in which systems are made up of sub-systems that have the same generic organisational characteristics.

Building on the systems and complexity theories and the dictionary meaning of agile (adjective), we can look at an agile organisation (or a business) which is able to move quickly and easily, able to think quickly and clearly to the changing environment.

According to the Agile Business Consortium (2016)[16]

An Agile business is an organisation that can respond quickly and effectively to opportunities and threats found in its internal and external environments (be they commercial, legal, technological, social, moral or political).

Mckinsey (2015)[17] conducted extensive research on this subject and have provided a definition of an agile organisation and defined its key characteristics. An agile organisation has a highly productive operating model that fluidly reconfigures towards opportunities that create value.

> Truly agile organisations, paradoxically, learn to be both stable (resilient, reliable, and efficient) and dynamic (fast, nimble, and adaptive).

To master this paradox, organisations must design structures, governance arrangements, and processes with a relatively unchanging set of core elements – a fixed backbone. At the same time, they must also create looser, more dynamic elements, that can be adapted quickly to new challenges and opportunities.

McKinsey's research and an analysis by Columbia Business School professor Rita Gunther McGrath, concluded that high-performing companies were both extremely stable, with certain organisational features that remained the same for long stretches, *and* rapid innovators that could adjust and readjust their resources quickly.

McKinsey's research[18] highlighted some important findings:

a   Highly ranked practices amongst Agile organisations:

  1   Role clarity and operational discipline – ability to balance fast action and rapid change, on the one hand, with organisational clarity, stability, and structure, on the other
  2   Innovation and learning – top-down innovation, capturing external ideas, and knowledge sharing
  3   Motivation – meaningful values and inspirational leadership

b   Three core organisational areas where balancing this tension between stability and flexibility is critical:

  1   Organisational structure – which defines how resources are distributed
  2   Governance – which dictates how decisions are made; and
  3   Processes – which determine how things get done, including the management of performance

Taleb[19] (2013) introduced the concept of Anti-Fragile as an interesting perspective to look at organisations. Agile (or Anti-Fragile) organisations thrive and grow when exposed to volatility, randomness, disorder, risk and uncertainty. Taleb describes Anti-Fragility as beyond resilience or robustness which becomes better when faced with the above situations.

7.4 EMERGENCE OF BUSINESS AGILITY

This section will explore the emergence of Business Agility from two perspectives. Business Agility as we know today, emerges from the world of Agile methods primarily from IT/software development. This has further evolved into the term 'Enterprise Agility' or even 'Enterprise Business Agility', both being used interchangeably.

Organisational Agility as a concept has been around arguably before prevalence of Agile methods, with an aim to develop organisations that are responsive, flexible, adaptable and resilient to fast changing external and internal business environments.

Business Agility emerged from the world of Agile software development where organisations and IT teams were looking to build on the successes of these practices and considered scaling them at the enterprise level. This was often fraught with issues of the wider business not understanding and appreciating the change required to move towards an Agile way of working.

In the last decade, terms such as Agile Transformation and Lean Transformation have emerged as well as scaling frameworks such as SaFe (Scaled Agile Framework), LeSS (Large Scale Scrum), DA (Disciplined Agile) Framework, Scrum of Scrums and Nexus. The merits and demerits of these different approaches can be debated endlessly. They all have a similar origin in Agile philosophy, values and principles and with the same intended purpose – to help and enable organisations, teams and individuals adopt Agile practices at an enterprise level. We will explore some of these approaches in more detail in the following sections.

2.4.1 THE FRAMEWORK FOR BUSINESS AGILITY

The Framework for Business Agility[20] was launched by Agile Business Consortium[21] in October 2016. This framework enables a business focus for Agile at a scale that is unmatched in the current market. It is suitable for profit, not for profit, government or charity, and enables a business to be more responsive to customer and market needs, thrive in an increasingly dynamic, demanding and resource constrained world. The Framework for Business Agility embraces the philosophies and principles that underpin all Agile methods.

2.4.2 DOMAINS OF AGILITY

At its simplest, *Business Agility is the capacity and willingness of an organisation to adapt to, create, and leverage change for their customer's benefit*. This simple statement exposes the dramatic shift in mindset needed for agile organisations. Where and how you respond to the market is reliably more predictable than how the market responds to you.

The Domains of Business Agility:[22] A simple model consisting of 12 interacting domains across four dimensions centered around the customer. The domains in each dimension are equally important, necessary, and interrelated to each other. You cannot realise business success in an unpredictable market until you develop agility in each of these domains across all areas in your organisation.

Holbeche[23] (2015) proposed a model with various component activities of organisational agility and resilience. It outlines key inputs and anticipated outcomes and has people and culture at the heart of the model which permeate all the quadrants.

- Inputs required to build agility and resilience

  Capabilities
  Resources and enablers
  Activities and interventions

- Outputs and effects

  Speed and innovation
  Immediate, intermediate, and long-term results

There has been notable work done by McKinsey, Meyer, Laloux, Birkinshaw[24] and many others where the focus has been around exploring Organisational Agility in a holistic way. The terms 'agility' and 'agile' have found their way in a non-IT sense to mean being flexible, adaptable, and open to change.

The Agility Shift model by Meyer[25] (2015) is the intentional development of the competence, capacity, and confidence to learn, adapt, and innovate in changing contexts for sustainable success.

According to Meyer (2014), agile leaders, teams, and organisations are effective because they are able to quickly become aware of the current reality and reframe the challenge to reveal its opportunities. Organisations that prioritise agility also prioritise ways of being, thinking, and acting, that enable agility and create space to move, reflect, and respond effectively.

The Agility Shift can be further understood through the Relational Web, which is a personal and system-wide network for mutual support, coordination, and resource and idea sharing.

The Relational Web helps with two essential needs in the midst of uncertainty and volatility:

a   Sense making (comprehending what is happening/has happened)
b   Meaning making (discerning and determining the significance of what is happening/has happened)

Developed by Robertson (2015),[26] Holacracy is a self-management practice for organisations and has been adopted by over 500 organisations.[27]

Holacracy empowers people to make meaningful decisions in pursuit of an organisation's purpose. It offers an alternative model to other self-management practices which lack the rigour needed to run business effectively. Holacracy claims to bring structure and discipline to a peer-to-peer 'operating system' that increases transparency, accountability, and organisational agility.

According to Birkinshaw and Ridderstrål (2015, 2017),[28] the concept of adhocracy was first proposed several decades ago as a flexible and informal alternative to bureaucracy; they have attempted to redefine the concept to distinguish it from bureaucracy and meritocracy model of an organisation.

By emphasising experimentation, motivation, and urgency, adhocracy aims to provide a necessary complement to progress in advanced analytics and in machine learning, which automates decisions previously made through more bureaucratic approaches. Key features of an Adhocracy are:

1   Decisive (and often intuitive) action over formal authority or knowledge
2   Decision by experimentation – to try a course of action, receive feedback, make changes, and review progress
3   Flexible governance – can be created and closed down very quickly, according to the nature of the opportunity
4   Motivating people through achievement and recognition – centres on giving people a challenge and providing the resources and freedom they need to surmount it over extrinsic rewards

Fredric Laloux), in his ground-breaking book *Reinventing Organisations*, presents an emerging organisational model – The Evolutionary Teal Organisation[29] which comes with three important breakthroughs.

- Self-management. Teal organisations operate effectively, even at a large scale, with a system based on peer relationships. They set up structures and practices in which people have high autonomy in their domain and are accountable for coordinating with others. Power and control are deeply embedded throughout the organisations, no longer tied to the specific positions of a few top leaders.
- Wholeness. Teal organisations invite people to reclaim their inner wholeness. They create an environment wherein people feel free to fully express themselves, bringing unprecedented levels of energy, passion, and creativity to work.
- Evolutionary purpose. Teal organisations base their strategies on what they sense the world is asking from them. Agile practices that sense and respond replace the machinery of plans, budgets, targets, and incentives. Paradoxically, by focusing less on the bottom line and shareholder value, they generate financial results that outpace those of competitors.

Laloux's book provides an evolutionary and historical view on how every time humanity has shifted to a new stage of consciousness it has also invented a radically more productive organisational model.

This model is similar to Holacracy, described earlier, and has been adopted by a number of organisations with great success. It heavily draws on the work of several thinkers, including Clare Graves, Ken Wilber, Jenny Wade, Don Beck, Robert Kegan, and Jane Loevenger.

Kotter (2012),[30] introduced a new framework for competing and winning in a world of constant turbulence and disruption. He explains that traditional hierarchies and processes together form an organisation's 'operating system'. They do a great job of handling the operational needs of most companies, but they are too rigid to adjust to the quick shifts in today's marketplace.

He argues that most agile, innovative companies add a second operating system, built on a fluid, network like structure, to continually formulate and implement strategy. He calls this a 'dual operating system' – one that allows companies to capitalise on rapid-fire strategic challenges and still make their numbers.

This second operating system is underpinned by five principles:

1   Many change agents, not just the usual few appointees.
2   A want-to and a get-to – not just a have-to – mindset.
3   Head and heart, not just head.
4   Much more leadership, not just more management.
5   Two systems, one organisation.

Peter: A comprehensive explanation/history lesson I think you will agree – my thanks to Parag for this exceptional insight.

I particularly concur with the statement that, at its simplest, Business Agility is the capacity and willingness of an organisation to adapt to, create, and leverage change for their customer's benefit.

As Parag has said, this simple statement exposes the dramatic shift in mindset needed for Business Agile organisations.

All of which brings me back to my decision to entitle this book, and all associated speaking, discussions, and teachings, 'Business Agile'. We could talk many terms, I myself have also used the concept of the Adaptive Enterprise, but I am settling on 'Business Agile'.

Now join me in a journey to explore this 'Business Agile' world and how you can help your organisation navigate the new normal and be successful.

NOTES

1 Mack, O., Khare, A., Kramer, A. and Burgartz, T. (2016) *Managing in a VUCA World*, Springer International Publishing, Switzerland.

2 Mack, O., Khare, A., Kramer, A. and Burgartz, T. (2016) *Managing in a VUCA World*, Springer International Publishing, Switzerland.

3 *The Economist* (2009) 'Organisational Agility – How Business Can Survive and Thrive in Turbulent Times', The Economist Intelligence Unit.

4 http://dictionary.cambridge.org This is the source for all definitions.

5 Agile Manifesto (2001) 'Manifesto for Software Development'. Accessed on 19th June 2017 at http://agilemanifesto.org/.

6 Scrum is an agile framework for developing, delivering, and sustaining complex products, with an initial emphasis on software development, although it has been used in other fields including research, sales, marketing and advanced technologies.

7 Dynamic systems development method is an agile project delivery framework, initially used as a software development method. First released in 1994, DSDM originally sought to provide some discipline to the rapid application development method.

8 Crystal method is an agile software development approach that focuses primarily on people and their interactions when working on a project rather than on processes and tools.

9 Feature-driven development is an iterative and incremental software development process. It is a lightweight or Agile method for developing software.

10 The Pragmatic Programmer: From Journeyman to Master is a book about computer programming and software engineering, written by Andrew Hunt and David Thomas – focused on avoiding duplicating code, information, or documentation. Every piece of knowledge should be a single, unambiguous, authoritative representation within a system.

11 Rigby, D.K., Sutherland, J. and Takeuchi, H. (2016) 'The Secret History of Agile Innovation', *Harvard Business Review.* Accessed on 19th June 2017 at https://hbr.org/2016/04/the-secret-history-of-agile-innovation

12 Goldman, S.L., Nagel, R.N. and Preiss, K. (1994) *Agile Competitors and Virtual Organizations: Strategies for Enriching the Customer*, John Wiley & Sons, Chichester, UK.

13 Source: https://en.wikipedia.org/wiki/Complex_adaptive_system

14 Hoverstadt, P. (2008) *The Fractal Organisation: Creating Sustainable Organisations with the Viable System Model*, John Wiley & Sons, Chichester, UK, Kindle Edition.

15 Anthony Stafford Beer was a pioneering British consultant and leadership theorist who is best known for his theories regarding management cybernetics, and how to apply them to human organisations.

The most famous of his theories was his Viable System Model (VSM), developed over a period of 30 years of observation of various different businesses and institutions.

16 www.agilebusiness.org

17 Aghina, W., De Smet, A. and Weerda, K. (2015) 'Agility: It Rhymes with Stability', *McKinsey Quarterly*, accessed on 28th May 2017 http://www.mckinsey.com/business-functions/organisation/our-insights/agility-it-rhymes-with-stability

18 Aghina, W., De Smet, A. and Weerda, K. (2015) 'Agility: It Rhymes with Stability', *McKinsey Quarterly*, accessed on 28th May 2017 http://www.mckinsey.com/business-functions/organisation/our-insights/agility-it-rhymes-with-stability

19 Taleb, N.N. (2013) *Antifragile: Things that Gain from Disorder*, Penguin Books, Kindle Edition.

20 Source: www.agilebusiness.org

21 ABC (2016) 'The Framework for Business Agility Overview', Agile Business Consortium. Accessed on 4th July 2017 at https://www.agilebusiness.org/resources/white-papers/the-framework-for-business-agility-overview

22 Leybourn, E. (2020) 'Domains of Agility'. Accessed on 11th May 2020 at https://businessagility.institute/learn/domains-of-business-agility/

23 Holbeche, L. (2015) *The Agile Organisation: How to Build an Innovative, Sustainable and Resilient Business*, Kogan Page, London, UK.

24 There has been notable work done by many authorities, we will meet some of them shortly, where the focus has been around exploring Organisational Agility in a holistic way.

25 Meyer, P. (2015) *The Agility Shift: Creating Agile and Effective Leaders, Teams and Organisations*, Bibliomotion, Kindle Edition, Brookline, USA and CGI (2016) 'The Agile Cultural Shift: Why Agile Isn't Always Agile', CGI Group.

26 Robertson, J.R. (2015) *Holacracy: The Revolutionary Management System that Abolishes Hierarchy*, Penguin, London.

27 Source: http://www.holacracy.org/

28 Birkinshaw, J. and Ridderstrål, J. (2015) 'Adhocracy for an AGILE Age', *McKinsey Quarterly*. Accessed on 28th May 2017 at http://www.mckinsey.com/business-functions/organisation/our-insights/adhocracy-for-an-agile-age and Birkinshaw, J. and Ridderstrål, J. (2017) *Fast/Forward – Make your Company Fit for the Future*,Stanford Business Books, Stanford University Press, Stanford.

29 A Teal organisation is an emerging organisational paradigm that advocates enabling employee autonomy and adaptation as an organisation grows. It was introduced in 2014 by Frederic Laloux in his book on *Reinventing Organizations: A Guide to Creating Organizations Inspired by the Next Stage in Human Consciousness*, Nelson Parker.

30 Kotter, J.P. (2012) 'Accelerate!', *Harvard Business Review*. Accessed on 18th August 2017 at https://hbr.org/2012/11/accelerate

RECOGNISING THAT YOU ARE IN A BUSINESS AGILE WORLD

This is going to be a really short chapter.

You are in the Business Agile world. Accept it. Deal with it. Move on.

The only reason you might not think you are, is if you are in a state of denial, because the world today is VUCA, and the only response to a VUCA world is to become 'Business Agile'.

As I said. Accept it. Deal with it. Ignore at your peril.[1]

I could write another two or three thousand words to argue and convince you but really there should be no point after recent times. So, I will not waste our time.

You are in the Business Agile world and need to take the guidance in this book on how to deal with it.

NOTE

1 Is that even possible in this post Covid-19 world, and was that a Black Swan I just saw?

IS IT POSSIBLE TO UN-VUCA THE VUCA WORLD?

4.1 THE BIG FOUR QUESTIONS

I always think it is best to start with some questions and in the VUCA world there are, I believe, four really big ones to ask:

1   'How can we prepare ourselves to move at the speed required and to be flexible in our approach in order to meet volatility with stability?'
2   'How can we prepare ourselves to accept uncertainty and to move this towards certainty?'
3   'How can we understand what can't, apparently, be viewed?'
4   'How can we have all the information that we need to make insightful (and rapid) decisions and how can we gain advantage from wisdom across the organisation to use this well?'

The VUCA world challenges an organisation in a number of ways, and you may well recognise one or more of these in your own organisation:

- Presenting boundaries for planning and policy management
- Confounding the ability to make decisions in an accurate, relevant, and timely manner
- Confusing the recognition of issues that impact, as well as the consequences of such issues and any associated actions, along with their variables
- Clouding the true interpretation of opportunities to grow
- But it is possible to break out of this VUCAish existence by:

- Breaking boundaries through collaboration
- Which will also provide the means to make decisions in an accurate, relevant and timely manner, utilising the power of the many, the hive mind and the power of the many
- Distribute the management of issues that impact, as well as the consequences of such issues to the 'network' – in other words to decentralise in order to manage effectively
- All of which will free you, your colleagues, and your organisation to see the real opportunities to grow

4.2 HOW TO DO THIS (SHORT VERSION)

Collaboration comes from decentralisation, from a softening of rigid governance, from opening the channels of mass communication and contribution and from demonstrating that your organisation truly values the input, thoughts, and contributions of all.

Being able to gain from this 'mass collaboration' and the 'power of the many' then decisions can be made in a relatively accurate, mostly relevant and opportunely timely manner – but also applying a 'you'll never know everything so just make a decision it's better that no decision' kind of way.

At the heart of this is the enormous capability of a truly aligned team (or teams) sharing their combined wisdom and expertise in an open and supporting, collaborative way.

Gain further from this community and distribute the management of issues that impact, trust in the people – it's not easy and you may need some help, but it can be done and it will be powerful, so trust your team, your group, your organisation.

Underpin all this with an agile approach to change.

And add in significant servings of unlearning what needs to be unlearnt in order to be free to see the real opportunities to grow.

4.3 HOW TO DO THIS (LONG VERSION)

The following chapters offer the longer version of the above under the headings of:

- Collaboration
- Teaming

- Agile Project Management
- Unlearning
- Meeting Complexity with Simplicity

And of course, a summary to act as your reference guide on your journey out of the VUCA wilderness and into the promised land of Business Agile.

COLLABORATION

5.1 WE ARE (ALREADY) SOCIAL

> We human beings are social beings, we carry into the world as a result of others' actions we survive in dependence on others, whether we like it or not there is hardly a moment of our lives when we do not benefit from others' activities. And for this reason, it's hardly surprising most of our happiness arises in the context of our relationships with others.
>
> The Dalai Lama

We are social, there is no fighting this, we are fundamentally social creatures.

And as a result of that, this stretches into the business world, of course.

We have taken to this modern social (tool) world seamlessly, painlessly, easily and we consume more and more of it on a daily basis. No one 'sold' us this technology, no one trained us in this technology, no one really helped us with all becoming experts in social media (maybe apart from a quick YouTube video view and a quick question to the youngest person in the room). No, we just got on with it.

I spend most of my time on LinkedIn these days and if you're on LinkedIn and we are not connected yet then send me an invitation to connect I will happily accept that connection.

I also do some blogging and podcasting, and I'm on Twitter as well, but I know there are hundreds of other social platforms (that my kids use[1]), a bewildering array of social media platforms, open and ready for our personal lives.

We've gone the whole 'tweetfacelinkblogpodoogle'[2] route and we get it, there's just been no learning curve really, we kind of teach it to ourselves for the most part.

And we have just taken to it, duck to water style.

But in the business world it is perhaps a little bit harder, although certainly recent circumstances around the world have probably accelerated the whole adoption and digital transformation.[3]

5.2 SOCIAL COLLABORATIVE MANAGEMENT

Maybe it is best to start off with a couple of definitions because this is about social collaborative management, and therefore a social collaborative manager. So what do I mean by that and what does it mean in bringing this into the workplace?

Q   How do you define social collaborative management?

A   When teams can enjoy the benefits of both the structure of the formal and the capability of collaborative management together with the rich online features available in today's online collaboration (social) environments, the results are immensely powerful. It is a balance between that traditional centralised, top-down, authoritative model and the decentralised, bottom-up, collaborative model.

Social collaborative management is based upon the philosophy that, in order to be successful, most collaboratives need the structure of a plan, together with suitable governance but with the value-add of the associated emergent collaboration and coordination tools and techniques.

Q   And what is a social collaborative manager?

A   I have found, over and over again, that collaborative managers know what is expected of them, and they want to do a great job, and they want to remove the inefficient practices they have to work with each day. The common access to open information through collaborative 'social' tools allows for faster impediment removal and higher levels of inter-collaborative activity to remove such inefficient practices.

Therefore a 'social collaborative manager' is someone who both recognises this and embraces it for the greater good of the power of the many. The time, I believe, is very much now, I think, for this to be hugely successful across all organisations. And the heart of it, is this concept of a mass collaboration.

5.3 MASS COLLABORATION

The idea of mass collaboration is that you don't just rely on the two people down the road from you in the office, you don't rely on, you know, one or two experts here or there, and you don't rely on a small group of people. And these days you most certainly do not rely on gathering people into a physical meeting.

Now you have the ability to reach out and gain this collaborative input from hundreds, possibly thousands of people, but let us be realistic and say within your full and complete team.

With the ability of this modern technology, and this modern way of working, this collaborative world, you can engage so many more people, and it's an incredibly powerful thing when it happens.

Admittedly it can be a scary thing as well and some people just don't always take to it immediately, but stick with it, and the results will amaze you (trust me).

5.4 THE HIVE MIND

One thing I love about this is the concept of the hive mind.

There are many examples out there but I'm going to pick on one which I think will resonate with most people and simply represent the art of the possible.

There was a piece of research done by an AI company and Oxford University here in the UK. They got a group of fans passionate about football.[4]

About 50 people came together and individually they were asked to predict the results of the football results in the Premier League in England and over a number of weeks. As you no doubt know, the English Premier League is one if not the best in the world with some amazing teams and players. This is the world of teams like Manchester United, Manchester City and Liverpool!

Of course, in any sports league, you know that there are teams that are currently hyper performing or teams that are really struggling and so sometimes results are pretty easy to predict, but when you get the mid table teams it's not always so easy and then, of course, there's always the surprises.

After ten weeks of this experiment the accuracy of their predictions and these knowledgeable but amateur football fans got it right around about 53% of the time. More right than wrong of course, but only marginally better than tossing a coin, so nothing to write home about really.

What happened next is that they re-ran the experiment, but the second time, instead of them individually predicting the results, they got the group to collectively predict the results. To come to a consensus.

The result? Well what they saw was an enormous increase in accuracy, up to 72% correct.

Now I know which approach I would want to use if I was a betting man.

This is the concept of the hive mind which brings together a group of people with knowledge and with understanding, and collectively they will come up with ideas, an answer, a solution, whatever you have tasked them with.

In *Drive: The Surprising Truth About What Motivates Us* Daniel Pink[5] explains that everything we think we might know about what motivates us is probably wrong.

He puts forward a core concept of motivation called the 4 Ts; in which people want autonomy over their 'Tasks', over their 'Time', over their 'Team', and also through their 'Technique'. The absence by design or other of this autonomy has bad consequences for performance and motivation.

And conversely of course if you want maximum motivation then you have to give people the 4 Ts.

Looking at the 4 Ts we might perhaps conclude that there is little that even a social manager can do in two of these – 'Tasks' and Time' – and perhaps that is correct but an open channel of communication within the team in even these areas might offer up alternative thoughts that might be beneficial to the team and the work objectives.

But in the other two – 'Team' and 'Technique' – there is ample room for social tool driven benefit. Tools and social media can allow for greater engagement 'within', 'around' and 'about' the project which leads to greater team performance and engagement. And as far as technique is concerned it is the manager's role to advise on the 'what', but it is the subject matter expert's role to define the 'how', and here again social tools and media can add to this through greater speed of information exchange, higher levels of engagement and wider validation of what is 'best' in each situation.

5.5 THE COLLECTIVE OBJECTIVE

I love this particular story.

There was a teacher, and the teacher was working on an exercise with their class. What they got the class to do was to blow up a balloon, and when they had a nice brightly coloured fully inflated balloon, the teacher got them to write their name on the balloon in black marker pen, big and bold and easy to see.

Then the teacher got all the balloons, put them in the corridor and gave them a really good mix up.

The teacher then said to the children, 'Go and find your own balloon please'.

Now I am sure you can imagine the chaos of school kids, charging around kicking balloons all over the place, trying to find their name on their balloon, throwing down the wrong balloons without care and probably making a lot noise at the same time.

At the end of five minutes, apparently, nobody had found their own balloon, the balloon that they blew up originally, wrote their name on proudly.

The teacher then told everyone to 'Stop' (and probably calm down and be a little quieter at the same time).

The teacher then gave new instructions to the children. They said 'I want you to pick up the balloon next to you and when you look at the name on that balloon go and find that person and give them their balloon back.

Within two minutes everybody had the balloon that they had written on back in their hands.

Of course, the point about that is when there's not chaos, when you are not working as individuals, then you can achieve some amazing results and do it in an amazingly fast time.

5.6 A WARNING NOTE

So, social is good, I believe, social is great and all things collaborative and social should be encouraged.

A word of warning though.

There was a ship that was commissioned in the UK at a cost of £300 million.

The brief was 'The new royal research ship will be sailing into the world's iciest waters to address global challenges that affect the lives of hundreds of millions of people, including global warming, the melting of polar ice, and rising sea levels' (Jo Johnson, Science Minister (at the time)), 'And we want a name that reflects the serious nature of the science it will be doing'.

And so, they asked the great British public[6] to think up names.

What the people came back with was 'Boaty McBoatface'.

This name had more votes than every other name put together and the government suddenly realised the error of their ways, and in this instance, the government unsurprisingly said, 'No, we are not going to call it Boaty McBoatface'.

They, in fact, named the vessel 'The Sir David Attenborough,'[7] an incredibly esteemed and well known and respected naturalist.

As a consolation prize, the name Boaty McBoatface was instead given to a small, yellow autonomous underwater vehicle, capable of traveling long distances under the sea ice to collect data, which forms part of the ship's research equipment.

The ceremony to formally name the Sir David Attenborough took place at a shipyard in northwest England, and Kate, Duchess of Cambridge, pressed a yellow button to activate a lever that smashed a bottle of champagne on the ship's hull, in accordance with maritime tradition.

Prince William, when ushering Sir David Attenborough to speak after him, drily noted 'It is my immense privilege and relief to welcome Sir David Attenborough, rather than Boaty McBoatface, to speak'.

However, on board that ship is a submersible, and that submersible's proud name is Boaty McBoatface, so they did actually consider the greater public.

Perhaps, just a humorous story, perhaps it's about the power of the people, but don't be surprised at some of the results that can come back. They may make you smile, but mostly they will benefit you and your organisation.

NOTES

1 These are the 'gang of nine': Ash, Jen, Tor, Georgia, Adam, Sam, Ellie, Scott, and Jaz

2 OK, made up word but you know what I mean.

3 The 'current' (when writing this book) joke is who is most responsible for accelerating digital transformation – CEO? CIO? CTO? Or Covid-19 – answer is obvious, Covid-19.

4 To be clear I am talking about English football here, proper football.

5 Daniel H. Pink is the author of six provocative books about business and human behavior. His books include the long-running New York Times bestsellers *When* and *A Whole New Mind* — as well as the New York Times bestsellers *Drive* and *To Sell is Human.*

6 When has that ever not worked out well?

7 Sir David Frederick Attenborough is an English broadcaster and natural historian. He is best known for writing and presenting, in conjunction with the BBC Natural History Unit.

TEAMING

Peter: Team performance management is a passion of mine along with the associated team building, project teaming, team performance measurement and re-teaming.

I have always lent heavily on the 'people' side of projects, change, transformation, and leadership, believing that such focus is at the true heart of success.

Simon Sinek's[1] performance vs trust video is a compelling example of true team membership.

I reached out to Bentzy Goldman[2] to provide his thoughts in this area based on his extensive experience in the world of project team analytics and performance management.

6.1 PROJECT-TEAM PERFORMANCE

6.1.1 INDIVIDUAL > TEAM > PROJECT-TEAM

When I think of 'performance management' I think of something quite different to what most people associate with it – – which is typically the horrid performance review including long forms, ratings and of course the dreaded feedback sessions.[3]

To me, performance management is not management at all but rather performance 'enablement'. It starts at the very beginning of a team's formation and is a fluid process throughout their lifecycle. It does not happen on a certain date and at a certain time, it's always happening, and I don't mean that spyware software that tracks time on devices and applications with the occasional creepy picture snapped (where's Snowden when we need him?).

What I mean is that at all times, managers and colleagues are looking for ways to help each other be better and reach their goals, both as teams and individuals. The evaluation process itself is a part of it, sure, but it needs to be a more holistic approach to not just understand the 'how' of performance but looking at the 'why'. It is much easier to assess how a team or individual is performing, it's not as easy to understand the deeper reasons behind why their performance is both low and high.

There is a multitude of research on what makes up a high performing team and yet few focuses on how to action the research into their teams from the very beginning of assembling them. Executive teams seem to get more attention in this area, and I think a huge opportunity is missed when it comes to project teams specifically which rely so much on collaboration and teamwork to be successful.

Both management methodologies and technology vendors (which usually follow the former) have not evolved or innovated much in this space and specifically when it comes to teams. These vendors will advertise 'Team performance management software' but when you actually use their products you quickly realise that such products are built around the old system – the individual. The fundamental issue here is that the very make-up of these systems is built and designed around individual performance and *not* true team performance.

This presents an obvious mismatch between the way people work (in teams) and the way they are motivated and evaluated (as individuals). There are many problems that arise when applying the individual system to a team.

1   It fosters unhealthy competition between team members.
2   It creates conflicting agendas and priorities within the team.
3   It doesn't provide performance data on a team level.

Furthermore, the project team, compared to all other team types is completely unique in its make-up and the way it executes work. This uniqueness requires its own personalized approach to performance management. In an ideal world different team types would have their own unique approach to performance management as there really is no one size fits all approach (contrary to popular belief). Unfortunately, at the moment (July 2020) both the traditional and modern approach to performance management are applied the same to all teams within the organisation. To my shock, even the most prolific and fully project orientated companies in the world operate on the individual performance model. To reiterate, their **entire** organisation (aside from admin and facilities) work in teams and specifically project teams. I will talk more about 'modern performance management' shortly, for now let's look at what performance management means in project management.

6.1.2 PERFORMANCE EVALUATION

Evaluating performance on an individual level becomes tricky in a project team where the results of the project are dependent on multiple people and external factors. In a project where there are many dependencies in the workflow this could lead to a situation where someone is evaluated incorrectly because their performance is partially dependent on someone else's performance, which obviously creates inaccurate performance data and breeds resentment within members of the team.

6.2 WHAT DOES PROJECT PERFORMANCE MANAGEMENT MEAN NOW?

Well you only have to ask the next project manager you meet, and they will tell you with confidence. I'll save you the time – it's a lot of abbreviations like; CPS,[4] WBS,[5] EVM[6] and double worded nouns like 'risk management'.

Hang on, but what about the people?

Well that is my point.

Project management as a profession and practice is hyper-focused on the 'process', the methodology, how a project ought to be run, yet a very small aspect of project management training speaks to the human element of projects, and, if it does, the very terminology of it could easily mistake humans for machines. As crucial as planning and 'process' are, it is often so emphasized and prioritized that the very ones executing the plan (according to the process of course) are neglected. A project team is a people team, it's as simple as that and if you're going to manage a project you ought to know how to manage people.

This lack of people training in project management clearly has an effect on future project success, often leaving PMs learning the hard way throughout their careers. High performing teams execute high performing projects, it's not rocket science. It is time for a shift in mindset and culture when it comes to the people side of projects. An investment that can and will pay off, as demonstrated in every other area of business. Invest in your people, develop them and you will in return have a higher engaged and higher performing organisation.

On top of raising awareness and improving training materials (by ingraining the people aspect into PM training), in order to sustain this shift it is essential to hold PMs accountable to the people element of their projects as much as they are evaluated on other metrics. Incorporating the results of their team's engagement and performance into their reward structure is a smart strategy to ensure that the focus is prioritized.

One of the obstacles that has caused this oversight, I believe, is the ambiguity surrounding who is actually responsible for the people management in a project team. Is it their functional manager? Is it HR? It's not the project manager surely, their job is to manage the project, not the people. The straightforward answer here is the same as my previous answers – people make up a project and thus it is the person in charge of the project. A functional manager may receive feedback at the end of the project on their subordinate's (gotta be a better word for that by now) performance yet they are rarely directly engaging and working with them throughout the project which makes it quite difficult to hold them responsible, or even have them filling out performance reviews.

6.2.1 MODERN PERFORMANCE MANAGEMENT

'Team performance' or rather 'team enablement' does not only consist of evaluating the performance of a team but rather it consists of every single part of the team's lifecycle from before they are formed to after they are dismantled. The entire process of forming–norming–performing should contain its own elements of performance enablement, consistently looking to understand and improve. The famous Kaizen method[7] can and must be implemented when it comes to people as much as process.

Over the last few years there has been a major and growing shift from 'traditional performance management' to 'modern performance management' or agile/continuous/real-time performance management, whatever you want to call it. It consists of a more fluid approach where performance is focused more on growth than scrutinisation.

It encourages more conversations or 'check ins' and much more frequently than once a year. A big emphasis is put on feedback and coaching which, when done right, has proven to stimulate performance and even improve retention rates amongst employees. Recognition is also now integrated into the culture and system of modern performance management, not recognition of poor quality work or missed deadlines (that we have plenty of from managers) but rather positive reinforcement in bite size moments throughout one's work week.

The science proves it, one of our most primal desires for acknowledgment and praise which when filled makes for a happy employee (for more on that science ask Mark Zuckerberg[8]).

6.2.2 WHAT PROJECT-BASED PERFORMANCE MANAGEMENT SHOULD LOOK LIKE

Conceptually and in practice everything surrounding performance in a project team should focus on alignment. Alignment of the people (sponsors, PM, team, stakeholders etc.) and alignment of strategies and goals. Everything else is commentary. Communication, clarity, resources, dependability, support, I can go on… At the end of the day EVERYTHING circles back to alignment and everything else is related in some way. Pay undivided and constant attention to it. Be creepy about it. Creepy as in persistently checking in on your team's clarity of agenda not rocking up at their houses at 2am with a big 'ARE WE ALIGNED' sign.

The thesis is, if you had a constant pulse on the alignment of your project team there should never be those surprises that creep up on you and threaten your project's success.

It's no surprise that the risk of misalignment is higher in agile teams, specifically product teams where requirements and needs change so frequently.

In order to prevent misalignment in the first place, it's important to understand what causes misalignment in project teams.

- Lack of clarity – On scope, process, roles and responsibilities and the project's purpose.
- Conflicting agendas – When leadership or individuals compete for personal gain.
- Conflicting objectives – When different business units have different desired outcomes.
- Lack of trust – From project leaders and between the team members themselves.
- Lack of transparency – From senior levels as well as knowing who's working on what.
- Communication breakdown – From sponsor to stakeholder to team member.
- Blurred lines of reporting – Not knowing who's who, overlapping reporting.
- Lack of empathy/Culture clashes – Lack of understanding of the needs and perspectives of individuals from different business units and cultures.

- Form teams that are small from the onset (consider personality/skills matching).
- Agree on methodologies and workflows. Use visual representation of how the project will be executed including and especially dependencies/handovers etc.
- Clarify expectations before the team starts the project. This includes outlining what success looks like and what metrics the team/project is going to be measured on.
- Define the purpose of the project and how it ties to organisational strategy.

- Digitise all requirements and resources to ensure everyone knows where to look for a piece of information if needed.
- Outline who is responsible for decision making and have a defined process for it which does not include too many people as this slows down decision-making speed.
- Identify what might go wrong before starting the project in order to be prepared ahead of time for all possible deviations. This includes potential 'blockers', people who are known to challenge authority and struggle to collaborate with others effectively.

6.3 CONTINUOUS ALIGNMENT

Prevention is all well and good but how do you ensure and drive continuous alignment?

- Accountability should be sustained through the use of project management tools and frequent updates between the team calling for completed and upcoming tasks.
- Continuous clarity as goals and priorities shift, constantly communicating changes in priorities as well as adjusted roles. It's critical for the team to know who to go to for what.
- Transparency throughout the project not only fosters alignment but also increases trust. Holding secret senior level meetings isn't going to help the executors drive your strategy if they don't even know what it is.
- Over communicate to not just the team but also stakeholders at every step of the project, never leaving things open for interpretation. Keep comms in public channels even if you think others don't need to know something it may just be helpful for them.
- Frequent check-ins are essential, commonly in the form of stand-ups and retros. 1on1 check-ins are important to identify blockers and provide support on an individual level.
- Real-time reporting not just on binary metrics like 'tasks completed' and budget but also on team performance using pulse surveys and micro-reviews.

- Listen to the people who make up your project, they are likely to have ideas on how to increase efficiency and provide insights on challenges which may not be visible to you.

Last but not least, some sources of misalignment could have a positive impact on the project as they provide different perspectives. Therefore, look for opportunities, not just threats!

Marco Perezzani. PMI[9]

6.3.1 WHAT DOES ALIGNMENT LOOK LIKE?

How do you know when you've achieved alignment?

Well it's very simple, if you had to ask your team one question: 'What is the purpose of this project and what does success look like?' and 90% of them answered correctly you're already well above average. If however you get 60% or worse 40%, you've got some digging to do. On a more abstract level if you've ever seen a murmuration of starlings it embodies the pinnacle of what team alignment should look like. It is the ultimate form of synergy and agility combined. It's also a beautiful sight to see and watch.

Still need convincing?

From a bottom-line perspective, the Workforce Intelligence Institute's[10] research shows that when employees are aligned and focused, they positively affect the company's financial performance.

This starts with setting the vision for your project – the team's north star which guides everyone in the same direction, no matter what road they take.

Always coming back to the 'why' (yes, I know cliché). But it works!

The clarity of your end result at the beginning determines the probability of achieving it.

Yes, even in agile projects where iteration is anticipated and encouraged, there can always be a north star which will guide your team to success. For example, our product has changed countless times from when we first designed it. but the vision statement remained the same and thus the product and her beloved team were able to focus on solving the one problem they set out to, no matter the angle. (Perflo's vision statement is this: Enable project teams to achieve higher project success.)

The first major element of this approach is to make it a proactive process and not reactive (that exists already). So instead of a post-project review, try a pre-project review. Focus on lead measures vs lag measures. The fundamental of performance management includes setting out a goal or KPIs (key performance indicators) and on a certain date assessing whether we reached that goal.

Which makes very little sense. Why wait till the end of a project to evaluate its performance?

The technology exists to make this process seamless and not require constant meetings and include long forms with checkboxes and ratings. It's automated, intelligent and acts as a virtual aid to project managers as opposed to 'another app' which demands increased overheads and data input. Proactive performance management consists of defining what success looks like and what metrics matter for your project well before it kicks off. This process should be collaborative including not just project sponsors and stakeholders but also the people executing the project.

If they don't know and agree on what success looks like how are they to help achieve it?

These success measures should constantly be measured by gathering both quantitative and qualitative data from systems and humans. Research has proven that when teams collaborate on goal-setting right from the onset they are more likely to achieve those goals. In addition, teams that hold each other accountable to those goals throughout the project will have higher results.

And the second element is that it is continuous and real-time.

This means it's not date dependent. The obvious benefit of this is early-stage detection of potential bottlenecks and areas that need attention as they happen. Yes, there is an element of this that is human capital risk management which should be done at the very beginning of projects but it is virtually impossible to predict human emotions, behaviours and influences in advance, which is why keeping a constant pulse on your team is vital in ensuring project success.

And the third and final element is matching team performance with organisational strategy and company values.

This kind of seems obvious but, whilst that is true, it (many times) doesn't actually happen.

It seems that every organisation understands the importance of setting goals, but we all need goals that align employees to both project team and to business organisational objectives.

Everyone should be working to achieve the overall strategy, and aligning the goals that will deliver this strategy will put everyone on the same page and all working in the one direction.

Simply put, if your organisation isn't aligning these goals then outcomes will be significantly impacted (and not in a good way).

6.4 HR IN PROJECT MANAGEMENT

When it comes to HR and project teams, there seems to be a substantial disconnect.

I've spoken to both HR and project management professionals and they both share this sentiment. It seems odd that talent management is out of the picture when it comes to managing and developing talent simply because the operating structure of that talent differs to the norm.

It's not my intention to scrutinise HR departments on this but I haven't seen much awareness or knowledge of how project teams actually work within their organisation.

When you think of how much money and risk is involved in large scale projects, you'd think there would be a dedicated talent team focused on the people enablement of project teams.

Granted some projects only last a few weeks and the time for development is limited however being a part of the process of forming project teams and supporting them can have a hugely positive impact on the results the team produces. The role of HR in projects needs a fresh perspective and it should be designed around supporting project managers and enabling team productivity and boosting morale. There are proven factors that are seen within high-performing teams like 'psychological safety', which aren't considered by project leads and it's not their fault because it's not something they've been trained on, but this is an area where talent management can come in and facilitate. Especially in project teams which require innovation and efficiency, creating a safe environment where input from all team members is actively welcomed has proven to enhance team performance and increased results.

The role of HR when it comes to project teams should extend to the early stages helping to match skills and personalities to assemble an all-star team.

Again, there is a multitude of research around structuring high-performance teams.

Evaluating skills throughout and after the project is vital to ensure the right people are put on the right projects and project managers are continuously being upskilled in low performing areas (like people management). When matching people with projects, skills matching is only one element of it, in this new Gen Z world of work where passions and meaning are prioritized, ensuring that people are working on the projects they care about will become more and more relevant and has already proven to increase the talent retention rates within organisations that focus on this.

It's no surprise, it's basic social science that dictates – the more you care about something the more effort you will put into it and the more ownership you will take of its results and impact.

6.5 REWARDS AT A TEAM LEVEL

If we are evaluating performance on a team level now, it would only make sense to reward on a team level. This is a relatively progressive approach in the world of rewards and compensation. Until now it has been very much individual based, yet with the growing shift to team-based work across more and more business units, the individual approach becomes less and less relevant.

Team based rewards need to be approached in a very calculated and thoughtful way as there can be a few potential negative side effects that come with them. For example if there is a low performer in the team who held the project back but the project was still a success despite this and the team qualifies for a collective bonus – the rest of the team would naturally be resentful that this 'slacker' is taking home a bonus when they know the reality of their contribution to the team. The traditional way of avoiding this is to have a 'bonus pool' for the teams based on the project's success and allocate from that pool to individuals on the team who made the highest impact (take caution however when determining this, even 360 ratings present inaccuracies in the data).

Furthermore, teams that work in a value chain of teams to complete a project could argue why *their* team made the project a success and *they* should receive a higher bonus etc. Essentially there is no one size fits all approach to team-based rewards and on top of that cash is certainly not the only (or most effective) means of reward. The more frequent these rewards come the more motivated teams are throughout the project so consider frequency based on milestone or specific success metrics.

I think the culture of the organisation and the maturity of its staff will propel this process to either success or failure. It has the potential (when done right) to motivate and increase performance, yet on the other side of the coin it has the potential to cause hostility and disrupt performance within teams.

6.5.1   SHIFT TO A MODEL OF PROJECTS/TEAMS

We certainly know there is a major shift to project-based work and teams in general within organisations today and it won't stop gaining adoption. The very nature of hiring people and executing work has already changed from full-time workers to contract workers.

A lot of teams and specifically product development teams in service-based industries (or servicing internal stakeholders) operate like project teams yet don't always apply the best practice or assign PMs to manage the project. Yes, product owners, product managers are leading the team but are they leading the team or the product? Is the scrum master or agile consultant concerned about the human element or that sprints run on time and whether tickets are moved to the left or right side of the Kanban board?[11]

My point is, it's not just project teams that are lacking in focusing attention to the human experience and being part of the team.

6.6   MORE DATA. BETTER DATA. FASTER DATA

The data opportunity = APIs[12]

More data isn't always an advantage, if the data isn't insightful or actionable (or worse it's insightful but too late) its value diminishes along with its relevance. Having the right data at the right time enhances the speed and quality of decision making and in the world of agile, nothing is more indispensable. Organisations have always looked to data in order to learn, understand and ultimately increase performance, on both an individual and organisational level.

People analytics market is growing exponentially, and greater attention is being paid to the value of data. Example: 'HR Analytics Market Size Worth \$6.29 Billion by 2027', Grand View Research, Inc.[13]

People data on project teams has until now been extremely limited, if existent at all, the value of this data has been untapped and as such it calls for greater attention. This data can help management to ensure projects are on track at an early stage and detect any issues which may creep up. Furthermore, the power of this data lies in its ability to increase the probability of success of future projects.

When team performance data is captured in real-time throughout the project there is the opportunity to learn and act instantly to the insights available, yet as more and more projects across the organisation are measured, the insights become richer and even more valuable. A part of this data is important to understand more deeply the root causes of both low and high performance, what makes a project team successful, and how we can assemble high performance teams in the future. Knowing what factors are important to monitor and drive throughout future projects will undoubtedly increase the project success rates. Using this data to find correlations specific to your organisation's project types and objectives has the potential to enable predictive intelligence on project success right from the onset.

Something that any PMO and project sponsor would pay big bucks for.

6.7 ACTIONABLE

So, what can you practically do about all this?

Here are some steps you can take today to make your project organisation more human and thereby increase team performance:

1   Incorporate effective people enablement in the training of project managers and PMO teams.

2   Include talent managers in the process of project team planning early on and throughout your project.
3   Embed team performance management into the very system and process of your project management methodology.
4   Use technology to measure and increase performance of your project team.
5   Seek to constantly understand, learn and improve on the factors that influence your project team's performance and alignment.

Peter: My thanks to Bentzy for these words.

As noted project team performance management is a passion of mine along with the associated team building, project teaming, team performance measurement and re-teaming, so excited that this is absolutely a critical foundation for the new normal and the world of Business Agile.

Time to wake up Change Leaders, wake up Program/PMO/Project Team leaders, wake up anyone leading any team in fact, and HR leaders – let's talk today!

NOTES

1   Simon Oliver Sinek is a British-born American author and motivational speaker. He is the author of five books, including *Start With Why* and *The Infinite Game*.
2   Founder and CEO of Perflo – Project Team Analytics: https://www.perflo.co/
3   I am yawning already (Peter).
4   The critical path method, or critical path analysis, is an algorithm for scheduling a set of project activities. It is commonly used in conjunction with the program evaluation and review technique.
5   A work-breakdown structure in project management and systems engineering is a deliverable-oriented breakdown of a project into smaller components.
6   Earned value management, earned value project management, or earned value performance management is a project management technique for measuring project performance and progress in an objective manner.
7   Kaizen translates as change for good or improvement (kai – "change" and zen – "good"). This is a mindset and practice of continuous improvement through innovation and evolution.
8   OK, so this guy probably needs no introduction or explanation but, just in case, Mark Elliot Zuckerberg is an American media magnate,

internet entrepreneur, and philanthropist. He is known for co-founding Facebook, Inc. and is very, very, (keep going), very rich.

9 Personal interview with authors.

10 Workforce intelligence can be defined in several ways, and it already exists in some form at most companies. Essentially, it is intelligence on employee data, behaviour, and patterns that helps to create comprehensive and accurate data sets over time.

11 Kanban is a lean method to manage and improve work across human systems. This approach aims to manage work by balancing demands with available capacity, and by improving the handling of system-level bottlenecks.

12 API is the acronym for Application Programming Interface, which is a software intermediary that allows two applications to talk to each other.

13 https://www.grandviewresearch.com/

AGILE PROJECT MANAGEMENT

Peter: As a supporter of Agile and Hybrid project management (each situation lends itself to a particular approach is my personal opinion), I recognise that an underlying 'agile project management' ability and culture is a strong foundation for becoming Business Agile.

In this instance I reached out to a good friend who is an expert in this area, Emma Sharrock.[1]

Emma is one of Australia's leading Agile practitioners, with over ten years' experience, leading and coaching Agile teams.

7.1 INTRODUCTION AND CONTEXT

Agile emerged as a way of working to assist organisations, teams and individuals in adapting to the increasingly fast-paced change the world is experiencing. First, it changed the way software was delivered. Then it transformed how projects were delivered. Agile is now impacting the whole of organisations from technology to HR, Finance, Internal Audit, Procurement and more. Agile projects are continuing to outstrip traditional projects in their ability to deliver business outcomes, bringing the whole organisation on the journey of Business Agility. Agile has not only changed the way we deliver; it is changing the way we work and live.

Projects remain the ideal vehicle to deliver change and transform organisations. And the traditional approach to projects worked exceptionally well for a long time. Spend time upfront working out exactly what needed to be done, document it in detail, then build, test, go live. In an unchanging environment with no external influences, this is still a great approach. However, these environments no longer exist. We are now faced with a world that is changing faster than it ever has. As human beings, we are wired for linear, organic change. Yet we find ourselves faced with exponential change – something that is not only unfamiliar but difficult to comprehend. How difficult you ask? Imagine a chessboard – 64 squares in total. If you were to put one grain of rice on the first square, and two grains of rice on the second square, and continue to double the grains of rice on each square, what would you have? It starts off simply: 1, 2, 4, 8, 16, 32, 64, 128, 256, 512, 1024, 2048, etc. But if you keep going, the numbers get more difficult to do in your head. Keep going, and the numbers start to challenge a basic calculator.

The final square would have 9,223,372,036,854,780,000 grains of rice – more than two billion times as many grains as on the first half of the chessboard, weighing in at approximately 230 billion tons. According to data from Research Gate, somewhere in the region of 480 million metric tons of rice is produced every year globally.

Ray Kurzweil,[2] an American inventor and futurist, coined the term: 'second half of the chessboard'[3] when describing technology strategy and the exponential growth organisations are experiencing. Thomas Friedman,[4] in his book: *Thank you for Being Late: An Optimist's Guide to Thriving in the Agile of Acceleration*[5] agrees, and claims we are simply not ready for the exponential change we are experiencing now and are about to experience. We have not been ready for some time. Technology has overtaken us, and we need to *learn fast and govern smarter* to catch up. Our ability to do this will define our success and is at the heart of Business Agility.

7.2 PROJECT MANAGEMENT IN A WORLD OF EXPONENTIAL CHANGE

Traditional project management is a linear approach to solving problems and delivering business results. And quite an acceptable way of working in a world that is experiencing linear change. A traditional project is planned in detail, upfront with confidence that little will change in the time it takes to implement. And even when problems arise, they can be solved in a linear fashion. In a world of exponential change, projects cannot be planned in the same way, as those carefully documented plans will quickly become out of date, wasting valuable time. Also, when problems arise, they are more likely to be complex, with multiple options to solve, with each option having a range of impacts and risks to consider. This complexity means a linear approach to solving them will not work. A solution to yesterday's problem may not work today; conversely, something that failed to solve yesterday's problem may solve it today.

Just working harder, faster and/or smarter cannot overcome this. We need to create environments that enable us to learn fast so we can adapt. This means radically overhauling how we work and think.

7.3 BEING AGILE – THE AGILE MINDSET

Our outer world reflects our inner world. Our actions reflect our thoughts. Our values and beliefs are what create these thoughts. As humans, we are all unique, and our perspectives can bring both richness and conflict. And in a slow-paced linear world, the evolution of our beliefs and values could be taken care of by time. Think of the implementation of a new IT system in the 1980s. It might take a while for everyone to get onboard and transition from shuffling papers to entering data into 'the new computer'. But that is okay, this system was going to be around for 30 years, and the process it supported was not going anywhere. Eventually, everyone would be on board (or retire before they needed to get the hang of it).

Having worked on projects to replace 30-year-old systems like this, I can guarantee any new system is not going to last that long anymore. As for the processes that underpin it, they are changing rapidly, quickly outgrowing any 'new computer system'. As a result, we no longer have the luxury of time to adapt organically. This is where mindset comes in. By the time we reach the metaphorical second half of the chessboard, just working faster is not an option. We need to radically change how we think – which means looking at our values and beliefs. We're going to find a lot of values and beliefs that were perfect for the 'old world' where change happened more slowly, before smartphones, social media, and advertisements that know what we want before we do. And these values and beliefs, this mindset of ours, has served us well. But what worked in the past may not work in the future.

7.4 VALUES AND BELIEFS

Values and beliefs do not change overnight, but what we can do is examine our own beliefs and challenge ourselves with new beliefs. The following are useful beliefs to shift toward an Agile mindset:

- People work perfectly, and make the best choices available at any given time.
- The meaning of communication is the response you get.
- Every behaviour has a positive intent in some context.
- There is no such thing as failure only feedback.
- Problems are due to the system of work rather than any individual person.
- Decision making should be by the people closest to the work.
- Team outcomes get better results than individual outcomes.

Depending on where you are at with your Agile journey, some of these beliefs may seem uncomfortable for you. After working for over 15 years as an Agile practitioner, I can guarantee that the more we can believe statements like the above, the more success we will have adapting and thriving in this fast-paced world. These beliefs, and others like them, reflect what Carol Dweck[6] – author of *Mindset: The New Psychology of Success*[7] – describes as a Growth Mindset. People with a Growth Mindset believe their skills and intelligence can improve with effort. They believe they can change. So instead of rejecting one of these beliefs, ask yourself:

'What would you need to see, hear or feel for this belief to be true?'

Merely imagining the possibility opens your mind to the new. And even if this does not convince you, whether you like it or not, just by asking yourself this question, you have already started being more Agile. And taking this question into your next project or change initiative will make a world of difference.

7.5 THE LANGUAGE OF AGILE PROJECT MANAGEMENT

Agile Project Management is an approach via a series of steps that involves delivering value iteratively and incrementally throughout the project life cycle. Jim Highsmith,[8] the author of *Agile Project Management: Creating Innovative Products*[9], identifies the key stages of this lifecycle as:

- Envision
- Speculate
- Explore
- Adapt
- Close

On the surface, it might look like we are just re-labelling the traditional way of running projects until we look more closely at the language used. Words matter and they impact how we work and live. 'Speculate' replaces the term 'plan', showing that the future is uncertain and cannot be foreseen through a set, predictable plan. Teams no longer 'build' to a fixed design but rather 'explore' the concepts developed in the Speculate phase. This term permits them to adapt to changing conditions and challenge initial assumptions, continuously improving on the idea as they discover more – words matter. For a more in-depth insight into the power of words, look no further than the work of Masaru Emoto[10] who conducted double-blind experiments on water exposed to different words and studied the effects on the crystals through a microscope.

As you adopt a new way of thinking, it is important the words we use support us, not drag us back into old patterns. New beliefs need new thoughts. New thoughts need new words. These new words need to be backed up with new actions.

7.6 'DOING' AGILE

A friend of mine is pro-triathlete. To say she is fit is an understatement. Her routine consists of training every morning, seven days a week, apart from every third Sunday off. Weekday sessions start at 5.30am, and weekend sessions begin at 7am. As a casual triathlete for a few years, all I could do was marvel at her commitment. She told me one day after training that she hated early mornings. HATED them. She was not a morning person and early morning starts were not easy for her. I could not believe it. I asked her how she did it, and she simply said: 'I love the result I get from early morning starts, so I just get up. And to be honest, sometimes I'm up and out the door without my brain knowing what's happening.'

This is the perfect metaphor for Agile practices. Being Agile and adopting a mindset that is open to new beliefs is essential. But as you work on shifting how you think, you can also work on changing what you DO. And fortunately, that's a bit easier. But like my pro-triathlete friend, it takes commitment and consistency for those new practices to take hold. Because I can guarantee she did not start seeing the phenomenal results she has now after getting up early and training for a day, a week, or even a month.

However, for Agile practices to happen with commitment and consistency, they need to be focused on an outcome. One of the essential things an Agile project team does is plan collaboratively. But instead of focusing on detailed requirements, we start with why. We agree on the outcome of the project, why it is important and how the organisation will benefit from doing the work. And that outcome is written somewhere where everyone can see it.

7.7 INCEPTION

We also collaboratively agree on what success looks like in the context of that outcome, and we visualise it to ensure mutual understanding. This planning is often called Inception, and involves a range of people, from the senior leader sponsoring the change to the project team members doing the work. The first part of Inception focuses on the 'why' and 'what'. Activities include crafting the vision statement, understanding stakeholders, benefits, risks, agreeing on high-level outputs and getting clear on the definition of success.

By the end of this part, the team should have a clear understanding (and agreement) on why the project is so important, what they are going to deliver (at a high level), what they can trade-off and critical messages to share.

This part of Inception (and the next part too) can be challenging. Differing opinions are shared; arguments can happen. Underlying assumptions surface. 'Shadow work' brought out of the shadows. I once had a business stakeholder say of a project deliverable that was not at all related to the project vision: 'I was hoping it would accidentally happen'.

This uncertainty can make people believe that 'this Agile thing is not a good idea'. As Ken Delcol[11] says:

> 'The joy of iterative development is that if you are lacking a vision, it becomes obvious sooner than a traditional approach. A traditional approach creates the illusion that a vision exists for a number of months before someone figures out what is going on.'

The difficult conversations we have as part of Inception are the same conversations that happen in a more traditional project. They just come up later, when there is little that can be done apart from paying the penalty, whether that be in time, cost or sanity.

The next part of Inception moves to the 'how' and the team collaborate to flesh out the detail. High-level outputs are broken down into features and stories, and the team agrees on how they want to work together. The team will also collaborate to align their understanding of current and future processes, action plans for risks and estimate the work in the next level of detail.

By the end of this part, the team will not only have walls of post-it notes and index cards, they will also have a plan. They will know the features, new processes, priorities, estimates and risks. They will also have an agreed way of working together. They will be ready to work at pace.

Inception embodies the Agile value: Responding to change over following a plan. Inception activities create a plan of sorts, but the collaborative nature of Inception sets the team up to have a clear understanding of the project goal, guardrails, and considerations. In the process, the team get to know the work (and each other) well, and this understanding, coupled with strong working relationships provide the environment that enables the fast flow of work. And also, the swift resolution of problems. In the same way as it is easier to work with someone you have known for a while or have some kind of history with. Someone you trust. Building trust with a colleague usually takes time, but in the world of fast-paced change, we do not have that sort of time.

Inception builds trust without having to spend that time. Although Inception can take a week or more, this intense effort brings energy and momentum. By the end of it, the team is a true team, ready to get stuck into the work. Inception finishes with a showcase to share the plan so far to project stakeholders, a team retrospective to reflect on the process and how they worked together, and sprint planning for the first sprint. After that, the team gets on with the work. At the end of the first-time box, or sprint, the team pauses, shares the work they have done so far, reflects on progress and ways of working and plans the next sprint. And the cycle continues.

7.8 THE POWER OF FEEDBACK

A standout feature of the Agile Project Management framework is the presence of a feedback loops. Agile is a non-linear process, centered around iteratively delivering value, unlike the more traditional ('waterfall') approach that has set phases that happen one after the other. Admittedly, Winston Royce,[12] when he designed the traditional project management process, did advise there should be a feedback cycle between build and test, but this was missed by mainstream project management. Projects continued to work their way through phases, with 'stage gates' at the end of each phase, indicating the next phase could begin. These 'stage gates' generally centre around the completion of documents or approvals, rather than the delivery of anything valuable to the customer. The Agile PM process not only allows for change but expects it, accepting that change happens, and the feedback cycles ensure there is space for change in the process. The showcase, retrospective and sprint planning that conclude Inception not only share the plan and set the team up for success with their wider stakeholder group, but they also embed this powerful feedback loop early in the project.

7.9 BUSTING THE ILLUSION OF CERTAINTY

Imagine being shown a beautifully presented building plan, with every room sized to the closest millimetre, every underlying system described in detail, every section colour coded. It may even be laminated. How difficult would it be to suggest moving a wall or a bathroom? Such an exceptionally detailed plan gives the impression that everything has been extensively thought out. But has it?

Traditional Project Management gives certainty early in the project. That is because a lot of time is spent upfront working out everything that needs to be done. In detail. This extensive 'requirements gathering' phase produces a detailed description of everything that will be done over the course of the project. It is probably professionally bound with a fancy cover page and a ten-page Executive Summary. The problem with this is that it gives the illusion of certainty. The detailed project plan is accurate at that moment in time. The problem is that the moment work starts, and change influences the project, the plan will need to change. It is so much harder to change a detailed plan than it is to change a high-level plan, with just enough created to start work. Think about anything you have created, from writing a document to preparing a presentation pack to building a house. At what point is it easier to make changes? When it is still in the early stages – a draft or high-level plan. The time spent in Inception is not spent estimating time and cost to the smallest detail (and documenting it), but rather putting in place a system of work that enables the project team to work at pace, and adapt quickly to change. The post-it note plan on a wall moves to the team's physical and/or virtual work area, where the team refers to it daily. Work is shared often, providing opportunities for new ideas to be considered, and issues to be resolved.

The most significant mindset shift to embrace when thinking this way is becoming (more) okay to share unfinished work. The project stakeholders review a wall of post-it notes rather than a 67-page bound document. The post-it notes can move if needed. Everyone can visualise easily how the project might look if something changed – whether it be a priority, a size or a new scope item. It is much easier to move a post-it note around than to re-write a paragraph in a document. However, it is also challenging to share something you have not finished. Especially if you are the kind of person who likes things to be 'just right'. If you are going to adapt to the fast-paced world we find ourselves in, you are going to need to learn to be okay with sharing your unfinished work and taking feedback. I am talking to all of you out there with your perfect PowerPoint presentations that you have pains-takingly put together over a period of time that is far too long to comprehend. You know who you are!

We make this shift by embracing the feedback loop. Your first draft, your first attempt – the first output you share – will not be perfect. However, the feedback you receive will enable you to create something so much better than what you could have done on your own. That is the power of collaboration.

7.10 THE POWER OF TEAMWORK/COLLABORATION

Collaboration is an essential part of Agile ways of working. Collaboration is at the heart of Agile project planning and con-tinues to be critical in getting the work done. The team will not only share work early and often, but also collaborate to do the work. Seeing multiple people sitting at a single screen is not unu-sual. While it may seem wasteful to have two people looking at one thing, experience has shown this results in work getting done faster and at a much higher quality. It also results in the team learning continuously. Both value and learning are embedded into every Agile team. This concept of 'pair programming' emerged from Extreme Programming (XP),[13] and it extends beyond creat-ing code. It even works for that perfect PowerPoint presentation.

Perhaps when a team is simply 'building' to a pre-defined detailed set of requirements, collaboration would not be as cri-tical. People could work in their individual siloes, producing individual pieces of work to be assembled at the end. However, when the team is exploring, aiming to create value more often, collaboration is critical. The impact of a team member working in isolation even if only for a day can impact the team's ability to deliver value fast. Conversely, the impact of two people sit-ting together for a few hours can be game-changing. In Agile, we create an environment for game-changing results every day.

7.11 BE COMFORTABLE WITH BEING UNCOMFORTABLE

For many traditional project managers, the thought of not having a detailed Gantt chart[14] and a substantial project requirements document to refer to can seem unnerving. When our goal is Business Agility, where value is continuously delivered and to a high standard through collaboration, these relics of the past are security blankets at best, and wastefully unnecessary at worst. They were designed to solve problems of the past, not of the future. With access to a washing machine, you would not choose to wash your clothes by hand in a river.

Fortunately, there is a short cut to this as well. If the thought of losing your security blanket makes you too uneasy, simply create an artefact that reflects the plan that gives you the comfort you crave – a spreadsheet, a Gantt chart, a document. Do not subject the team to it – this is for you, not them, and they have enough to do. Also, if you are going to create this security blanket, you must do something else. Do something that makes you uncomfortable. Anything. Take a dance class, go to a Meetup you have not gone to before, do improvisation. It does not have to terrify you (if you are scared of heights perhaps give bungee jumping a miss for example), it just needs to put you out of your comfort zone.

The more you spend time outside your comfort zone, the more your comfort zone grows, and so do you.

7.12 CERTAINTY AMID THE CHAOS

The Sahara Desert is the largest hot desert in the world, and comprises most of North Africa, covering 9 million square kilometres from the Red Sea in the east to the Atlantic Ocean in the west. Before the invention of GPS, people navigated safely across this vast expanse – how? Mileposts. Mileposts are 50-gallon oil drums full of sand with a flagpole on top. As you travel across the desert, you do not leave one post until you can see the next one. The long journey to traverse the desert is broken into short trips. An Agile sprint can be thought of a milepost of sorts – somewhere to aim when the whole journey is not in easy sight. And within the Agile sprint, there are even more mileposts – and these Agile events (sometimes called ceremonies) are designed to ensure the team stays on track and connected. I have found these events immensely useful in my Agile projects to not only stay connected to the team and the outcome, but also to give the team (and myself) a moment of certainty in a vast desert of unknowns. They provide a richness of information, knowledge, experience, and insights that no document (however thick and bound) can.

Sprint Planning: Every sprint, the team get together and decide what they are going to focus on for the immediate time period based on priorities. They collectively commit to the work via a series of conversations that uncover any hidden assumptions or misunderstandings.

The Daily Stand Up: Every day, the team get together to share what they have been working on, what they plan to work on, and any help they need. It is a short meeting where the focus is on the work to be done to achieve the project vision.

Team Retrospective: Every sprint, the team get together at the end and reflect on the work done, and how they have worked together. Finished work is celebrated, unfinished work is noted, and actions agreed to amplify the positives and address the negatives. These actions become part of the next sprint and are never more than a few to avoid overwhelming the team.

Sprint Review/Showcase: Every sprint, the team get together with their stakeholders to share work done so far. It is an opportunity for stakeholders to ask questions, give feedback or suggest changes. As stakeholders, it provides certainty that their needs are being heard. As a project manager, it is the ultimate stakeholder management and communication opportunity.

Backlog Refinement: Once or twice in a sprint, the project stakeholders and some team members will get together to refine the backlog. This session is an opportunity for the stakeholders to share the broader business context, shift priorities and advise any changes that will impact the project. A new requirement may emerge, a requirement may no longer be needed. It is also an opportunity for the team to understand the project priorities and the thinking behind them. Keeping with the theme of the feedback loop, the team will share the impact of any changes, even at a high level, and ask questions to ensure understanding; including which requirements are no longer priorities, and as a result, may not be done.

7.13 FROM JOB DESCRIPTIONS TO TEAM ROLES

In an Agile project, the outcome is the most important thing. Simply being outstanding at your job is not enough. We are often expected to flex outside our prescribed job description to achieve the project outcome, and our ability to do this is critical to getting results fast. This is why Agile projects have specific roles and responsibilities that might be different from a traditional job description.

A question that I get asked a lot is 'Where is the project manager in Agile?' There is no role called Project Manager in Agile practices like Scrum, but that does not mean that project management skills are not needed. They are just required in a way that transcends the 'old world' limitations of fixed roles, enabling us to adapt to fast-paced change. Your value is now derived from what you can contribute to the team to achieve the outcome, not your excellence as a Make Your Business Agile.

The key roles in an Agile team include the following.

> The Project Sponsor is ultimately responsible for the benefits of the project. They own the overall outcome and are selected as the Sponsor as they have the most to win when the project is successful, and the most to lose if it is not. They must have 'skin in the game' and be committed to the project's success. They champion the project and support the team by being available to answer questions and give guidance when needed.
>
> The Product Owner is responsible for prioritising the work and is either the project sponsor or an empowered delegate, who is available to the team on a daily basis to answer questions, provide context and generally ensure the team can move at pace. Rather than waiting until the next steering committee, the Product Owner will give in-the-moment input and troubleshooting support. The Product Owner is the voice of the customer and the business; however, they will engage stakeholders throughout the project for their expertise and advice. The more involved and engaged the Product Owner, the more successful the team.
>
> The Scrum Master facilitates the Agile process. The Scrum Master supports the team and ensures the workload is balanced and fair, as well as ensuring the Product Owner is aware of critical pre-requisite work that may not link directly to business value. Failure to do this work results in what is known as 'technical debt' and can bring an organisation to its knees if not considered. A healthy tension between the Product Owner and the Scrum Master is a good thing,

and any challenges are opportunities to learn, grow and enable high performance.

At the heart of the Agile project is the team. The team is a cross-functional, multi-disciplinary group of individuals who work to create an outcome much greater than the sum of its parts by collaborating to understand the work, share ideas and concerns and implement in the best way. They also are empowered to decide how much they can do in a sprint, therefore owning the work. This intrinsic motivation further enables high performance. A team should be as 'long-lived' as possible, meaning that rather than disband the team at the end of a project, keep them together to work on future work. They are already geared to work at pace and deliver exceptional outcomes. The term 'take it to the team' refers to bringing work to a team to work on, rather than assigning it to an individual.

A person with project management skills may play any of the above roles depending on their experience and interests; and depending on the size of the project may still play the actual role of the Project Manager, responsible for ensuring the project gets done. The Agile Project Manager focuses on providing an environment where the team can do their best work. This focus requires a lot of outward-facing effort to support the team in collaboration with the Scrum Master and Product Owner.

7.14 ENABLING BUSINESS AGILITY

Collaboration, sharing work, constant feedback and continuous improvement are core to Agile projects. And these concepts can be easily transported out of the world of the project into any team. The essential elements are a shared outcome to which they can all contribute, the belief that they can change, and the willingness to work together to do so. Being and doing Agile starts with the individual, is magnified by the team, and realised by the organisation. Imagine the power of teams, and 'teams of teams', all contributing to an organisation's most important goals. Organisations like Spotify, Amazon and Atlassian have proven this is possible. Our increasingly fast-paced world has confirmed that it is essential.

And it starts now.

In fact, it has already begun.

Peter: Thank you Emma for this clear and useful insight into Agile Project Management.

As Emma states, at the heart of the Agile project is the team, and this is so true and fits (perfectly) with the other key areas of collaboration and teaming that form the true foundation of a Business Agile enterprise.

NOTES

1 Please see Emma's full details in Chapter 12: 'My valued contributors'.
2 Raymond Kurzweil is an American inventor and futurist. He is involved in fields such as optical character recognition, text-to-speech synthesis, speech recognition technology, and electronic keyboard instruments.
3 The 'second half of the chessboard' is a notion put forth by Ray Kurzweil in 1999 in his book *The Age of Spiritual Machines* (Viking Press). He suggests that while exponentiality is significant in the first half of the board, it is when we approach the second half that its impacts become massive, things get crazy, and the acceleration starts to elude most humans' imagination and grasp.
4 Thomas Loren Friedman is an American political commentator and author. He is a three-time Pulitzer Prize winner who is a weekly columnist for *The New York Times*.
5 *Thank You for Being Late: An Optimist's Guide to Thriving in the Age of Accelerations*, by Thomas Friedman (Macmillan: USA, 2016)
6 Carol S. Dweck is an American psychologist. She is the Lewis and Virginia Eaton Professor of Psychology at Stanford University. Dweck is known for her work on the mindset psychological trait.
7 *Mindset: The New Psychology of Success*, by Carol S. Dweck (Random House, 2006).
8 James A. Highsmith III is an American software engineer and author of books in the field of software development methodology. He is the creator of Adaptive Software Development.
9 *Project Management: Creating Innovative Products* (Agile Software Development Series), Addison Wesley, 2004.
10 Masaru Emoto was a Japanese author and pseudo-scientist who claimed that human consciousness can effect the molecular structure of water. Emoto's book *The Hidden Messages in Water* published in 2004 was a *New York Times* best seller.
11 Ken Delcol is an expert in product development with extensive experience in both hardware and software development.
12 Winston Walker Royce was an American computer scientist, director at Lockheed Software Technology Center in Austin, Texas. He was a pioneer in the field of software development, known for his

1970 paper from which the Waterfall model for software development was mistakenly drawn.

13 Extreme programming is a software development methodology which is intended to improve software quality and responsiveness to changing customer requirements.

14 A Gantt chart is a type of bar chart that illustrates a project schedule, named after its inventor, Henry Gantt, who designed such a chart around the years 1910–1915. Modern Gantt charts also show the dependency relationships between activities and current schedule status.

UNLEARNING
A CRITICAL 21ST-CENTURY SKILL FOR ALL

Peter: It came as a late realisation, perhaps age does make you wiser, but I eventually realised that throughout my life, my career, there have been times that I have had to 'unlearn' what I have learnt in the past.

Learning, it seems, is not a never-ending summation of all that has gone before, but a series of step changes in understanding and knowledge.

As Albert Einstein said 'The world as we have created it, is a process of our thinking. It cannot be changed without changing our thinking.'

In this instance I was intrigued by the work of Barry O'Reilly[1] in the area of 'Unlearning' and, when I discovered another good friend was a leading advocate and educator in this area, I immediately reached out to Stephen Dowling to ask him to contribute a chapter on his specialism.

8.1 INTRODUCTION

It's 2:15pm on the 4th December 2015, and I'm sitting in a classroom doing an 'Agile Portfolio Management' course facilitated by one of the top agile consultants on the planet, 'Eric Willeke'.[2]

I'd heard about Eric from a few friends in the Agile community. He was a legend, a hard-core battle-scarred consultant who had worked with massive companies in the most challenging and complex of environments. Eric had been around from the very early days of the 'Agile' movement with Rally, and, if I wanted to get my head around this 'Agile' thing, I could do no better than learn from a guy like Eric.

As it was now just after lunch on the second day of the course, most people were struggling a little bit, but I was 100% engaged. For a day and half, I'd been listening to Eric, agreeing with what he was saying, and not being able to find fault with any of the logic, and downright common sense. However, I just could not connect it, and reconcile it with the traditional 'project management' world I'd been living and breathing for the last five years. How did it fit together? Did it fit together? How can I make sense of both of these worlds? Surely, they both had their place. I was finding it all very confusing, the multitude of different 'Agile' frameworks, methods, tools, practices and of course the terminology? I thought to myself, I've got to get to the bottom of this just for my own sanity!

At this exact moment in the class Eric shared an important insight that gave me another important piece in the jigsaw, and it allowed me to connect a few important dots in my mind. I suddenly felt violently ill. The reason for this was that, at this moment I genuinely felt that the last five years of my working life had been a complete waste of time!

Thankfully on reflection it wasn't quite as bad as this! During this last five-year period my mission had been to be become a recognised thought leader and one of the world's best trainers in project management. What I'd now realised was that there was a big gap missing in what I'd been doing, and the foundations upon which everything was built had to change and I could now see why. Yes, of course I could see there was value in what I had been doing, but it was only a part of a much bigger and complex puzzle. The world was changing and the way I was doing things was no longer good enough.

Also, and very importantly, I had some fundamental core mindsets (beliefs) which I had been operating against, which were now no longer appropriate and outdated, and I needed to evolve and unlearn these if I wanted to stay relevant. What I believed was most important had to change and quickly. This was a massive 'Unlearning' moment for me, which, I'll be very honest was extremely confronting and hard to accept. How much time and energy had I committed? The money I'd invested. The collaborative business relationships I'd spent time building.

This exact moment was the catalyst which sent me on a quite different path, and as a result my business today is completely different to what it was five years ago. This personal journey got me to realise firsthand the critical importance of unlearning. We've all got to be ready, willing and open to unlearn outdated mindsets (beliefs) when that's needed, no matter how hard it is. By not doing this, you run the risk of becoming irrelevant and faster than you might think possible!

8.2 LEARNING VS. UNLEARNING

I'll argue that learning is a given! The world is changing extremely fast and if we want to continue to stay relevant, we need to be able to continually learn new things, and it's extremely important that we see ourselves as continual learners.

However, while learning new things can be hard, the bigger problem I believe is actually unlearning the past. Barry's inspiration for writing his Unlearn book came from observing super smart and intelligent people. Yes, they could all learn new things, but what they all struggled with, was unlearning the past, especially if it had made them successful.

As humans we operate on autopilot most of the time. Our brains are wired to be record players and pattern seekers, so unlearning the past is actually not so easy to do!

Let me try to explain. Our brains are probably the most incredibly complex organs on the planet. Each is unique, and there are no two brains in the world exactly the same!

Our brain is made up of billions on neurons and trillions of connections.

In fact, I believe that each of our brains has more connections in it than there are stars in the milky way! Having said that there are two big dominant drivers governing how it behaves.

The first one is all about protecting us and keeping us alive, and the second one is about efficiency. The brain is our nerve centre responsible for managing and controlling everything, all of our bodily functions, so it will always want to conserve energy where possible to ensure it's best placed to keep everything going! The more things it can do automatically the better. The latest thinking in neuroscience reckons that 95% to 97% of what happens in our brain is automatic responses, based on our subconscious mind. Think about that for a second! So, knowing when you need to change, and how to break out of these ingrained mindsets, habits and responses is actually a big challenge for all of us.

If we need to learn a completely new way of doing something, which contradicts how we've done it in the past, then, to learn the new way, it's very important we're open to letting go of the old way first, otherwise, it will be very difficult to learn the new way, given that it fundamentally conflicts with our existing belief of how it should be done.

Unfortunately, we all have a natural 'sunk cost' fallacy in our knowledge and skills. If it's taken us a long time to acquire knowledge and skills, then it's not going to be easy to accept that these may have suddenly become obsolete, if the reality in which we operate changes.

Also, learning is not always an incremental and compounding activity. Sometimes we've just got to blow up and destroy old obsolete thinking and ways of doing stuff, so we can make way for the new and better way of doing it.

8.3 WHAT IS INLEARNING?

So, what exactly is unlearning? In his recent bestselling book, *Unlearn Let Go of Past Success to Achieve Extraordinary Results* (2018), Barry O'Reilly defines unlearning as follows.

> Unlearning is the process of letting go, reframing and moving away from once useful mindsets and acquired behaviors that were effective in the past, but now limit our success. It is not forgetting, removing, or discarding knowledge or experience; it is the conscious act of letting go of outdated information, and actively engaging in taking in new information to inform effective decision making and action.
>
> Barry O'Reilly

So, if our reality changes we've got to be open and willing to unlearn our old, outdated mindsets and behaviours if we want to ensure we will continue to stay relevant. It's not saying drop everything, it's just saying we've got to be ready to discard out-dated information if and when it happens.

It's very important to recognise that we actually do this already. As humans we're changing all the time. We do it unconsciously, when we have to, and where there is no choice, when we are forced to adapt in order to survive. My business had to change if I wanted to survive. My project management training revenue streams were drying up and I needed to move in a different direction, so I had no choice. I was forced to unlearn, so I did it!

So, if we do it already what's the big deal? The big difference now is that we are living in a world that is constantly changing, and it's going to keep doing this at an increasing rate, whether we like it or not. If we don't make unlearning something which we do on a much more frequent, consistent and deliberate basis, we run the risk of becoming obsolete and this could happen very quickly. What has worked well in the past may not be what will work well in the future.

To help us do this Barry O'Reilly has created a simple but very powerful system which he calls the 'Cycle of Unlearning'. To help us unlearn on a consistent and repeatable basis we need to use and apply this system. The more we do it, the more automatic and habitual it will become.

Step 1: Unlearn – The first step is to recognise WHEN and WHAT we need to unlearn.

Step 2: Relearn – The next is to figure out what we need to do different! If things aren't working, we need to think about, what new BEHAVIOUR might help us? If our existing behaviour was working, we would not need to unlearn, all would be good. In this step we need to design and create a small behaviour experiment for ourselves, which will help us to learn.

Step 3: Breakthrough – The final step is where we execute this behaviour experiment. See what happens when we do the small behaviour? Was it what we thought was going to happen? If so great, repeat and look to scale it up. If not, let's try something else. Pick another behaviour and go through the cycle again. The only way we'll achieve the breakthroughs we need is by doing these experiments on ourselves.

8.4 THE IMPORTANCE OF OUR 'MINDSET'

All that we are is the result of what we have thought. The mind is everything. What we think we become.

Buddha

What is a mindset? A setting of the mind. It goes to the very nucleus of every single individual. What do we believe? What is true? What is false? What is most important? What is least important? What is the right way to do things? What is the wrong way to do things?

When a baby is born does it have any beliefs? I'll argue no! Over our lifetime these mindsets (beliefs) develop, change and evolve based on our experiences, our teachers, our mentors, the training and education we get. What's very important to recognise is that what we believe will ultimately drive our actions and behaviours.

In order to be able to adapt to a changing world, organisations create new products and services. They also modify and add new features to existing products and services as required. What people don't often realise is that as humans, the most important things that we've got that can help us to adapt to our surroundings are our mindsets (our beliefs) and the behaviours we have.

Firstly, as humans we're not often conscious or aware of these mindsets (beliefs) that we're operating against, given the fact that, as we said before, we're operating on autopilot most of the time.

A fish swims in water, this is something which becomes ubiquitous to it, it does not even notice it! As humans what we've got to realise is that our mindset is like the water to the fish, this is something which is controlling our life, and how we think drives how we behave to situations.

The big danger is that we may be operating based on some old, outdated mindsets (beliefs) Secondly, we may see these as something which is 'fixed', non changeable.

I recently watched a Netflix documentary called 'The Game Changers'.[3] While watching this, a belief I have had got totally shattered. I had always believed that the best and most efficient way to get protein into our bodies was via animals (e.g. cows and chickens). In the documentary they asked one question which hit me like a ton of bricks, 'What does a cow eat?' If we get our protein from animals, we're getting it from the middleman! If we eat plants, we go directly to the source of the protein. Ever since watching this I've made a conscious effort to move to a more plant-based diet.

How many more mindsets (beliefs) do we all have, which we're operating against, which are false, outdated and obsolete?

8.5 UNLEARNING LEADERSHIP MINDSET

So now, we've realised that we have some outdated mindsets (beliefs) which we need to unlearn. How do we go about doing it?

First of all, you've got to realise that you cannot talk your way to changing your mindset, you've got to ACT your way to changing it.

Everything starts with our behaviour. Once we change our behaviour this will change our perspective of how we see things. This then, will impact our mindset, which of course will then affect our ongoing behaviour. This is why seeing ourselves as 'experimenters' is so important for the future. To help us unlearn and relearn we need to be constantly experimenting with our behaviours.

8.6 THE ROLE OF UNLEARNING IN ENABLING 'BUSINESS AGILITY'

Let me ask you a question.

Do you see organisations attempting to put in place a 21st-century digital capability, but layering it on top of old thinking, processes, and principles?

In my experience I see this happening everywhere.

The big problem is that these are fundamentally hugely different ways of thinking and working, and they cannot happily co-exist together. If this situation is allowed to co-exist in an organisation, it will ultimately result in a dysfunctional organisation! As a foundation we need to work on evolving a shared mindset (set of beliefs) across the organisation as to what we all believe is MOST important. Having this in place from top to bottom will drive common goals, synchronisation, and alignment, consistent organisational priorities, behaviours and actions, and will allow, a suitable 'culture' and 'system of work' to naturally evolve.

If our goal is to enable Business Agility and the establishment of healthy organisations (i.e. organisations that people want to work for and continue working for), that can sense and respond to a fast-changing external environment, they must embrace a 21st-century way of thinking and working (from top to bottom).

If you agree with this then I'm sure you can see that there is a considerable amount of unlearning needing to happen across all areas of an organisation (e.g. Board, Execs, Finance, HR, procurement, Risk and Compliance, Sales and Marketing, and even IT).

If this picture is allowed to continue, then I believe Business Agility is a pipedream, and an impossibility. What we say and what we do will be quite different. These poisonous gaps will lead to a toxic and destructive culture, and with it your hope of being able to attract and retain great talent.

8.7 CONCLUSION

> The illiterate of the 21st Century will not be those who cannot read and write, but those who cannot learn, unlearn and relearn.
>
> Alvin Toffler[4]

I genuinely believe 'Learning To Unlearn' is now a key skill needed by all, if we want to ensure we'll continue to stay relevant.

We have got to be incredibly careful and vigilant. If our reality changes, what has brought us success in the past may not bring us success in the future. In fact, it may end up being our undoing.

Our mindset (our beliefs) and our behaviours, are the most important weapons we've got at our disposal to help us adapt to a changing world. If we are able to continually learn, unlearn and re-learn then we will be able to adapt, survive and thrive.

Unlearning is especially important for our most senior leaders as they are the people who will have the power to change the fundamental 'system of work' within which people operate. Once they start unlearning outdated mindsets and behaviours, they will realise that their organisational systems need to change. How do we lead? How do we structure and organise ourselves? How do we assign, fund, and govern work? How do reward people? How do our management processes work? What metrics and measures do we use? If our 19th and 20th century organisational systems don't evolve then we've got a massive problem, and I will argue that the goal of Business Agility is an impossible dream.

As Deming once said, 'A bad system will kill a good person every time'. The overall system that's in place exerts a huge influence, and unless we can get this right, there is little hope of making a meaningful and sustainable difference. And the very best of luck with trying to attract and retain the best people!

Unlearning needs to be something that becomes automatic for all of us. It needs to become part of our operating DNA. By using and applying Barry O'Reilly's simple but powerful 'Cycle of Unlearning' on a very frequent basis, so that it becomes a habit, that we repeat automatically and instinctively.

If we can all 'learn to unlearn' on a continually and repeatable basis, we will have a critical foundational skill which will help us to navigate, and cope with our super exciting future!

Wishing you all the absolute best on your unlearning journey!

Peter: Thank you Stephen and I also believe that 'Learning to Unlearn' is now a key skill needed by all, if we want to ensure we (and our organisations) continue to stay relevant and survive (thrive) in this Business Agile world.

Learning, it seems, is not a never-ending summation of all that has gone before, but a series of step changes in understanding and knowledge, and that is a key lesson in itself.

NOTES

1   Barry O'Reilly works with ThoughtWorks, consulting with leading global organisations on continuous improvement using lean and agile practices and principles. His work includes *Unlearn: Let Go of Past Success to Achieve Extraordinary Results* (McGraw-Hill Education, 2018).
2   Eric Willeke, 'Unleashing the impact of agility', http://ericwilleke.com/
3   'The Game Changers' is a 2018 documentary film about the benefits of plant-based eating for athletes. It covers multiple success stories of plant-based athletes, references scientific studies, and touches on other arguments for plant-based diets that extend to non-athletes.
4   *Future Shock* (originally published by Bantam in 1970).

MEETING COMPLEXITY
WITH SIMPLICITY

A recent Siegel+Gale[1] study revealed that employees in simplified work environments are 30 percent more likely to stay at their jobs, because their time is spent on high-value work instead of endless meetings, reports, and emails.

I have long been an advocate for the KISS[2] approach in everything that I do and am involved in (i.e. have to personally experience).

> Leonardo da Vinci said, 'Simplicity is the ultimate sophistication' and Shakespeare wrote 'Brevity is the soul of wit'.
>
> 'Make everything as simple as possible, but not simpler' is also attributed to Albert Einstein, so I am in good company with this attitude.

The underlying principal behind my first book The Lazy Project Manager[3] was working smarter and not harder, and this can only be achieved through simple(r) application of thought, design, and action.

For Lisa Bodell,[4] in her book, *Why Simple Wins*, she asks leaders to imagine what they could do with the hours they waste, writing emails every day for example.

Her definition of simplification (the MURA model) involves the following four criteria:

1   Is it as minimal as possible?
2   Is it as understandable as possible?
3   Is it as repeatable as possible?
4   Is it as accessible as possible?

Try applying that to a process or two in your own organisation. The *Harvard Business Review*[5] noted

> Structural mitosis: In most large organizations, structural shifts are happening all over the enterprise, all the time. They may range from subtle changes in reporting relationships, to job moves accommodating personal preferences, to the establishment of a new unit or shared service centers. The steady accumulation of structural changes drives up complexity over time, in ways that sometimes go unrecognized.

Furthermore, the *HBR* article recommends 'Simplification as Strategy' for modern organisations.

> While none of the elements of simplification are particularly surprising by themselves, countering complexity requires integrating them into a multidimensional strategy. Though the elements each directly address one source of complexity, applying them separately may actually worsen the problem. For example, many companies have found that simplifying processes through large-scale enterprise systems—without addressing organizational structure, product offerings, and work behaviors—often leads to diminished rather than enhanced productivity. One-off efforts may interrupt established relationships, introduce unanticipated roadblocks, and create confusion over decision rights. A simplification strategy must also be treated as a business imperative—not a soft, "nice to have" virtue but a key contributor to bottom-line success.

Most businesses start simple and (increasingly) become complicated, but at the heart they are still simple.

For me, it is entirely sensible/logical/obvious/clear of the value of keeping things simple.

What sets great businesses apart from the rest is that there is that simplicity within, with a culture of KIS (let us drop the last 'S', we don't need it – do we?).

NOTES

1 Siegel+Gale is a global branding company headquartered in NYC.
2 KISS, an acronym for 'keep it simple, stupid' or 'keep it stupid simple', is a design principle noted by the US Navy in 1960. The KISS principle

states that most systems work best if they are kept simple rather than made complicated; therefore, simplicity should be a key goal in design, and unnecessary complexity should be avoided.

3 http://thelazyprojectmanager.com/*The Lazy Project Manager: How To Be Twice As Productive And Still Leave The Office*, 2nd edition (Infideas).

4 Lisa Bodell is the founder and CEO of futurethink, a company that uses simple techniques to help organisations embrace change and increase their capability for innovation.

5 'Simplicity-Minded Management' by Ron Ashkenas; https://hbr.org/2007/12/simplicity-minded-management.

SUMMARY
HOW CAN YOU PREPARE FOR A BUSINESS AGILE EXISTENCE?

10.1 TODAY'S BUSINESS DRIVERS

Driven by today's business uncertainty and accelerating pace of change, enterprises need to find a new way of operating which requires an adaptive and flexible way of delivering to their market demands.

These include:

- Collaboration not cooperation
- Taking advantage of the power of the many
- Social strategy and advantage
- Speed of decision making

As a business leader you should be playing a central role in creating the foundations of an adaptive and Business Agile enterprise, that is

- Outcome based – designing and building from the desired end result
- Collaborative – harnessing the power of the collective without the barriers of tradition
- Team focused – driving alignment and openness

Right now, business uncertainty abounds.

Forrester (The Adaptive Enterprise 2019[1]) expects this extraordinary uncertainty to continue.

The global economy shows signs of weakness and talk of recession grows louder; the US–China trade war is disrupting supply chains and impacting business investment; sophisticated cybersecurity threats target firms of all sizes and industries; automation of all kinds is changing work and the labour market; and firms and governments are being forced to ramp their investments in climate change adaptation more quickly than anticipated.

Then add in a heavy and painful Covid-19 experience[2] that is way from over and business uncertainty is higher than ever, globally.

Forrester further states:

Changing customer expectations and early stages of a new technology revolution are already making markets turbulent. These forces generate a level of volatility that creates acute risk – or extraordinary opportunity. The level of volatility places a premium on how well companies adapt. The market will reward adaptive enterprises and punish those unable to quickly sense and respond to the different forces playing out in the external market.

10.2 DISRUPTIVE INNOVATION

And what is powering much of that disruption? Think, Artificial Intelligence, Machine Learning, Augmented Reality and Virtual Reality, along with the Internet of Things and so on.

In business theory, a disruptive innovation is an innovation that creates a new market and value network and eventually disrupts any existing market and value network, displacing established market-leading firms, products, and alliances.

Right now, business uncertainty certainly abounds and demands the rise of the adaptive enterprise that operates truly at the Business Agile level.

Accenture summarised the opportunity in a recent article[3] on Tech Vision trends.

- **The I in experience**

  The enterprises that start building personalised, interactive, and shared virtual communities today can carry that success far into the future.

- **AI and me**
  Investing in AI and other tools that enable true human–AI partnership allows businesses to reimagine their workforce in the future.
- **Robots in the wild**
  While today's robotics leaders are filling new, pandemic-related roles, the ones genuinely thinking long-term are also building a more automated future.
- **Dilemma of smart things**
  Enterprises need to consider how they can introduce new features without overstepping. Failing to support these changes produces short-lived benefits.
- **Innovation DNA**
  Leaders who create agile and resilient innovation DNAs will be positioned to meet new needs and build new capabilities faster than ever before.

But technology is only part of the answer (and perhaps part of the, if not problem, at least the driver for change).

10.3 THE THREE KEYS TO THE ADAPTIVE ENTERPRISE WORLD

An adaptive enterprise can change its core value proposition to pursue the opportunities that volatility produces, whereas a non-adaptive enterprise is very much fixed in its ways and unable to change at any practical speed.

C-suite level leaders need to play a central role in building the capacities and capabilities of an adaptive enterprise, and to show the way.

Building a Business Agile, adaptive, differentiated enterprise will benefit from a set of clear and executable steps to allow leaders and teams to move forward in the right direction and to do this three keys should be considered.

10.3.1 KEY ONE: OUTCOME

The first key is being outcome focused – designing and building from the desired end result rather than from the start.

Rolls Royce 'Power by the Hour' is one of the best-case studies of an outcome-based business model. Traditionally Rolls Royce used to charge its customers based on support and maintenance of engines in commercial jetliners which was directly linked to number of technicians, fixing parts and the effort to do support and periodic maintenance. More than 15 years ago, Rolls Royce transformed its model to outcome and instead of charging customers for inputs and services like repairs, maintenance and the provision of spare parts, customers paid a fee per hour based on the number of hours of flying time for an engine.

What we're trying to say is that the process should serve the business – it needs to be defined, based on the outcome to deliver, just what's needed to accomplish the outcome. The process should not be defining how you work, nor should it overburden you with extra work if it's not required to achieve the outcome. Imagine a change world, for example, where project managers and project sponsors alike were rewarded on business benefits achieved rather that the delivery efforts of projects

THE ART OF OUTCOME THINKING OR ALIGNING THE FOUR OS

The Forbes article, 'Why Every Organisation needs Output Thinking'[4] states that you should be able to strip back every business to just four O's:

1   Objectives: Clearly defined, time-specific, measurable goals to focus activity within the business
2   Operations: Everyday tasks and actions
3   Outputs: Completed project deliverables that are 'micro outputs' at the individual employee level, and finished products that are 'macro outputs' at the organisational level
4   Outcomes: Experiences and benefits of those products, and the consequential growth for business by selling them

Too much energy is devoted to operations and outputs, and too little to outcomes – the goals, activities and deliverables that will best serve customers' needs. And that is the real business outcome to target: serving a real and valued need.

The mistake is to believe that creating an end product, for example, is the end of the story. As the late Steve Jobs[5] put it, 'You have to start with the customer experience and work backward to the technology. You cannot start with the technology and try to figure out where you are going to sell it.'

What is needed is a way of thinking that aligns consumer needs and producer activity: outcome thinking.

And consider, if you've created an outcome thinking 'muscle' that makes it second nature to focus on the value (as opposed to the process), then when the business drivers need to change, as they will, often –, you can easily tap into that 'muscle memory' and quickly re-align your teams and all their work to deliver against the new value driver.

That way the focus remains on the value and not on the change. Outcome Driven.

10.3.2 KEY TWO: COLLABORATION

The second key is being collaborative – harnessing the power of the collective without the barriers of traditional.

Collaboration at the conceptual level, involves:

- Awareness – becoming part of a working entity with a shared purpose
- Motivation – driving to gain consensus in problem solving or development
- Self-synchronisation – deciding as individuals when things need to happen
- Participation – being open to collaboration and expecting others to participate
- Mediation – negotiating to find a middle point
- Reciprocity – sharing and sharing in return through reciprocity
- Reflection – thinking, and considering alternatives
- Engagement – proactively engaging rather than sitting on the side-lines

It is not cooperation, that is different, collaboration is about shared objectives and outcomes, about trust – check out the John Spencer video.[6]

THE POWER OF THE MANY (HIVE MINDS)

One way to do this is to harvest the power of the 'hive mind'.

By harnessing the collective power, thoughts, experience, knowledge, and wisdom of the many, rather than the few, better decisions can be made. And by utilising the many business social technological platforms these more-inclusive decision-making processes can be faster than the more traditional 'meet/discuss/agree/act' physical meetings of the past.

One example, which we explored earlier in this book, of the power of this can be found in a study by researchers at Unanimous AI and Oxford University where a human swarm (large group) was used to predict the outcome of all English Premier League games. Results showed that individuals achieved a 53% accuracy, but when they were acting as a collective then accuracy rose to 72%.

We also considered the exercise that the teacher led with their students and the coloured, named balloons that showed that when everyone is clear on the goal (everyone finding their balloon in this instance) and what their role is in achieving it (helping each other), then the outcome is achieved faster.

Power is with the many it seems.

10.3.3 KEY THREE: TEAMING

The third and final key is being team focused – driving alignment and openness amongst all team members.

It is all about project team performance management, understanding the dynamics of team member interaction and working towards a common outcome at the highest levels of 'performance'.[7]

Team performance management is a passion of mine along with the associated team building, project teaming, team performance measurement and re-teaming.

I have always lent heavily on the 'people' side of projects, change, transformation, and leadership, believing that such focus is at the true heart of success.

> 'People are what make companies agile, not approaches, methodologies or tools.'
>
> Pedro Gaspar Fernandes[8]

The need to (re)engage distributed and virtually connected project teams in the 'new normal' requires leaders to

- Listen
- Clarify priorities
- Set a positive tone
- Reduce uncertainty
- Combat isolation
- Check on wellbeing

And right now, the call to action is to heavily focus on your teams and bring them back to a 'performing' state of mind and action through activities that will

- Re-build
- Re-engage
- Re-inspire

10.4 BARRIERS TO BEING BUSINESS AGILE

So, we have the three keys but what are the typical barriers in moving to this desired Business Agile culture?

1 **Hierarchy**
   The enemy of open collaboration is centralised hierarchical governance believing in a protectionist approach
2 **Traditionalism**
   The 'we have always done it this way' argument supported by referencing historical successes whilst ignoring future challenges
3 **Secrecy**
   The complete opposite to the 'power of the many' belief, operating on a 'need to know' basis only for those in power, controlling information and communications

4   **Enterprise system rigidity**
When the technology forces the behaviour of an organisation –
we may be in a 'new normal' but, when we return to work, it
will be under the process discipline of the old tools and existing technology so will anything actually change?

10.5 ADHOCRACY AND THE AGE OF AGILE

Professor Julian Birkinshaw, Professor of Strategy and Entrepreneurship at the London Business School has suggested that the
world is entering something he calls 'The Age of Agile'.

Organisations throughout history, Birkinshaw said in a speech
at the Global Peter Drucker Forum in Vienna Austria, were of
three types: bureaucracies, meritocracies, and adhocracies.

As a result we are now in the age of adhocracy where it is
about action, about getting things done, and done fast.

Experimentation and outcome achievement are key.

Business Agile is the approach of providing greater flexibility
and faster decision-making in the modern business world, a world
where organisations that aren't Business Agile will take longer to
succeed and be less flexible in this modern, demanding business
world, and fail at a faster rate potentially.

But that brings about a challenge with regards to supporting
this rapidly moving world of change driven through projects.

10.6 UNLEARNING

Unlearning what has been Learnt (and led to the Un-Adaptive
Enterprise).

It came as a late realisation, perhaps age does make you wiser,
but I eventually realised that throughout my life, my career, there
have been times that I have had to 'unlearn' what I had learnt in
the past.

Learning, it seems, is not a never-ending summation of all that
has gone before but a series of step changes in understanding and
knowledge.

As Albert Einstein said "The world as we have created it, is a
process of our thinking. It cannot be changed without changing
our thinking."

In this instance I, like Stephen Dowling, was intrigued by the work of Barry O'Reilly[9] in the area of 'Unlearning'.

The world is changing fast and if we want to continue to stay relevant, we need to be able to continually learn new things, and it's extremely important that we see ourselves as continual learners.

However, while learning new things can be hard, the bigger problem, we considered earlier on, is actually unlearning the past, letting go of the 'old' skills and opening our minds to the 'new'. Barry's inspiration for writing his Unlearn book came from observing super smart and intelligent people who could all learn new things, but what they all struggled with, was unlearning the past, especially if this is what had made them successful.

Think about that – do you ever let go of things that have worked for in the past? Madness, it is often said, is doing the same thing you did in the past and expecting different results.

10.7 START YOUR BUSINESS AGILE JOURNEY TODAY!

Change leaders today need to embrace this more social, decentralised, and collaborative world in order to succeed in the adhocracy age, the age of disruption innovation, the age of rapid evolution of business that we are well and truly in, right now.

The key is to get outcome focused, adjust the traditional rigidity of centralised governance, strip down the old, often overbearing and burdensome, processes, and believe, really believe; in the power of the people, acting through efficient teams, to deliver simple success in a time of complex demand.

Only the Business Agile will survive in this new world.

10.8 AND YOU DON'T HAVE TO DO IT ALONE

Get help with this unique journey of opportunity...

NOTES

1 https://go.forrester.com/adaptive-enterprise/
2 That flock of Black Swans (and yes Australia, I know a Black Swan is nothing special to you guys).
3 https://www.accenture.com/gb-en/insights/technology/tech-vision

4   https://www.forbes.com/sites/forbestechcouncil/2020/01/23/purposeful-action-why-every-enterprise-needs-outcome-thinking/#63e5ed11239e
5   Steve Jobs made this statement at the 1997 Worldwide Developers Conference; https://youtu.be/FF-tKLISfPE
6   https://www.youtube.com/watch?v=Gr5mAboH1Kk
7   Bruce Tuckman's Model of Team Development – 'Forming, Storming, Norming, Performing, and Adjourning'. See Tuckman, Bruce (1965) 'Developmental sequence in small groups'. *Psychological Bulletin.*
8   http://www.experienceagile.org/
9   https://barryoreilly.com/unlearning-business-innovation/

THREE FINAL THOUGHTS

This whole VUCA world and the road to Business Agility can seem quite daunting I realise, but I hope that the preceding words of some real experts (and myself) can give you hope – give you inspiration – give you the realisation that it is possible to succeed and thrive in this 'new normal' existence.

Three final thoughts from me that should be there in the back of your mind in the coming months.

- **Efficiency will kill in a VUCA world**
  Or rather the pursuit of perfection and trying to find out all the answers from all the data will kill you simply by creating 'analysis paralysis' and stop you making any decisions
- **Creativity will help you thrive**
  Instead open your mind(s) and work with your colleagues to collaborate effectively in a truly creative manner
- **Agility will allow you to succeed**
  And be 'agile' in every sense of the word, fight complexity, allow simplicity to flourish, and move fast everyday

Good luck!

Peter
October 2020

MY VALUED CONTRIBUTORS

As mentioned, I have relied heavily on people who just know more than me to provide the real detail and inspiration in this book.

You can read all of their amazing profiles below, and I urge you to connect to them all and talk 'Business Agile' with them in their various areas of expertise.

EVAN LEYBOURN

Evan is the Founder and CEO of the Business Agility Institute, an international membership body to both champion and support the next generation of organisations. Companies that are agile, innovative, and dynamic – perfectly designed to thrive in today's unpredictable markets. His experience while holding senior leadership and board positions in both private industry and government has driven his work in business agility and he regularly speaks on these topics at local and international industry conferences.

As well as leading the Business Agility Institute, Evan is also the author of *Directing the Agile Organisation* (2012) and *#noprojects; A Culture of Continuous Value* (2018).

EMMA SHARROCK

Emma is one of Australia's leading Agile practitioners, with over ten years' experience leading and coaching Agile teams. An accredited coach and trainer with extensive project and change management experience, Emma is passionate about working with people to transform the way they work and live. A former naval officer, Emma's role was safely navigating warships through treacherous seas. Her role now is not dissimilar. The sea has just been replaced by the rapidly changing business world. A world demanding more of our time and focus, as we navigate through the ambiguity and uncertainty.

Emma works with leaders and teams to navigate this unfamiliar environment by uplifting capability in ways of working, focusing on Agile practices, principles, and most importantly, mindset. These ways of working used to be considered 'nice to have' but are now critical for survival in this world of fast-paced change.

Emma has written two books, *The Agile Project Manager* (2015) and *High Performance Executive Leadership* (2019).

Emma genuinely believes that successful change is possible for anyone willing to shift their mindset. For anyone willing to implement small changes to make a big difference. For anyone willing to be Agile. Are you? www.theagileprojectmanager.com.au

BENTZY GOLDMAN

Founder at Perflo – High-Performance Project Teams

Start-up Junkie|Remote Work Advocate|Behavioural Science Nerd

Building tech for the future of work. www.perflo.co Project Team Performance Analytics. The new way to measure performance and increase alignment in your project-based teams.

STEPHEN DOWLING

Stephen has a strong background in both 'Traditional' and 'New' ways of working which enables him to help organisations to easily bridge this gap and take people and organisations on this extremely critical journey of evolution. He and his team pride themselves on being at the forefront of current thinking and continuously work to collaborate to build strong relationships with people and organisations who are seen as global thought leaders, allowing us to provide their clients with support and advice based on the latest best practice thinking.

ETM is a privately owned niche organisation passionate about helping people and organisations thrive in a fast changing and complex world.

This is done by not being afraid to challenge and disrupt traditional mindsets and thinking, working closely with their clients to design and build suitable high impact 'fit for purpose' programs, aimed at rapidly improving performance, solving real problems and helping to unleash the full potential of their people.

Stephen believes the continuous cycle of learning, unlearning and relearning is critical for future success. www.etm-unlearn.com

PARAG GOGATE

Parag is a an experienced, outcome oriented, certified business change, transformation, and improvement practitioner with a track record of developing and delivering strategic initiatives, IT enabled change, cultural changes, customer service improvement, risk management and business improvement initiatives.

He provides exceptional business acumen, change management, stakeholder engagement and team leadership – being able to see the strategic big picture and be equally comfortable to work at the operational level. He has the ability to manage uncertainty and complexity to deliver change and improvement across retail, facilities services, hospitality, technology, and not-for-profit sectors.

Acknowledged as an analytical, generative, and innovative problem solver, Parag has experience of full change life-cycle – from identifying business needs, designing strategies and plans, delivery of outcomes, change and transition management to benefit realisation.

He is highly experienced in the delivery of training and coaching programs with superb interpersonal, communication, facilitation, and presentation skills and an ability to manage stakeholders and client relationships in a positive influential style – from board, C-suite to operational level.

His practice is unique and trans-disciplinary, integrating fields such as agile, lean, systems thinking, complexity science, psychology and behavioural science, design thinking, coaching and other change program and project management good practices.

He is also a board member of the SCIO (Systems & Complexity in Organisations), co-lead of the Change Management Institute's Midland chapter, and co-founder of the London Business Agility Meet-up; he has published various articles, research papers and co-authored an *Introduction to Managing Change* guide.

One last time, thank you Evan, Emma, Bentzy, Stephen, and Parag.

INDEX

Ingram Content Group UK Ltd.
Milton Keynes UK
UKHW021301280423
420941UK00025B/692

9 780367 747084